PEPPER IN HER POCKET

THE STOVE AND STORIES OF A COUNTRY GRANDMOTHER

May wild flowers be the only weeds in your garden...

[signature]

Booklocker.com, Inc.
2007

PEPPER IN HER POCKET

THE STOVE AND STORIES OF A COUNTRY GRANDMOTHER

By

RaeAnn Proost

To those who came before us,
we celebrate your lives and offer our thanks.
We are awed by your faith and strength and courage.
We are proud to be descended from you.
We share your stories with those who follow us.
We rejoice in the recollection of names and faces, times and
places.

Ivie and Ainsworth

Ivie and Knight and Dorr

Ivie and Brasse

Ivie and Bell

Ivie and Erlandson and Proost

Ivie and Spellman

Ivie and LaMunyan

Memories are moments recollected.

Remembered sights, sounds, touches, and aromas are the facets
of an imperfect crystal.

My gratitude for the encouragement and support of family and
friends.
Special thanks to my editor, Meredith,
story sleuths Denny, Jeannie, and Gene,
photo technician, Michael,
and dear chefs, Gary and Melinda.
RaeAnn Proost
2007

PEPPER IN HER POCKET
THE STOVE AND STORIES OF A COUNTRY GRANDMOTHER

RAEANN PROOST

Journey Home

There is a place where I must go
That's snug within my heart.
I cannot know what waits for me,
Still it's time for me to start.
It's time for the journey home.

The memories come quiet and deep,
The moments that I'll always keep,
The memories that pull me there.
Prepare for the journey home.
It's time for the journey home.

Come away with me, come away and see
This place my memories' of:
The home that's made me what I am,
I remember laughter, love.

This is, you know, where I must go,
That place within my heart.
I cannot know what waits for me
Still it's time for me to start.
It's time for the journey home.

RaeAnn Proost

Inspired by the music of Michael Allen Harrison

Prologue

Little Grandma

My great grandmother Maria taught my grandmother, Mary Ann, to sew. Ever clever with the needle, Maria was quite the seamstress. She made her living fashioning fancies for the ladies. *Sunday go to meeting clothes* and wedding dresses were her specialties, and she tailored frock coats for the gentlemen. Mary Ann's seamstressing was more utilitarian, keeping her daughters in pantaloons, petticoats, and pinafores. She had a knack for altering hand-me-downs and appliquéing patches to coax yet another year's wear. For herself, to make her dresses last longer, she designed cobblers' aprons with pockets marching across the fronts. By end of day, those pockets would harbor strange collections of stray buttons, weeds with clumps of clinging soil, a *snot rag* or two, assorted hair pins, a page torn from a catalogue, a shiny agate, a note from a school teacher, lint. Errant pins, needles, and the occasional fish hook decorated the shoulder above her left bosom. Family and friends checked that shoulder carefully before sharing hugs.

Now my grandmother had one strong willed daughter and one naughty tongued granddaughter. Mary Ann took to carrying a bit of pepper in one of her apron pockets to catch the nasty tongues and words that erupted from those two. They never knew if they were being peppered with spice, particles of soil from her weed collection, or lint. All in good time, the wicked little tongues were tamed.

From the time I was born, my grandmother would mosey down to California to stay with our family, just after Christmas through May or June. Those months my little brother was booted out of our bedroom and landed on a cot in the dining room. His clothes and treasures were packed in boxes and grocery bags and stored beneath his makeshift bed. Grandma became my roommate. She took over two drawers, half of the closet, and my private life.

As a child I was mesmerized by the long hair she had never cut in all her years. Those silvery tresses hung past her backside. Occasionally she would overdo it with the rinse and her hair took on a certain shade of blue. How I wanted hair just like Grandma. I would wear it in the longest pony tail ever. She used metal curlers upon which she wound those tresses, to give them a bit of a wave about her face. The ends were twisted into a bun held with large silver pins high on the back of her head. She wore her hair in the same style from her late teens until the day she died. Over the years hints of pink scalp peeked through and the bun somehow slipped to the nape of her neck.

She bathed just once a week, she dared not dry her skin, but she cleansed her face nightly with cream from a big blue jar. I drank in the pleasant fragrances of menthol and eucalyptus as she admonished me to always take good care of my skin and use good tooth powder or baking soda on my teeth at least once a day. "And don't you never embarrass your Mama," she added.

At night, Grandma heaved a sigh as she stepped from her corset into her nightgown. Maria bought her daughter's first pale peach corset mail order when Mary Ann turned eighteen. Allowed no lip rouge and only a dab of vanilla behind each ear, the young woman was thrilled and felt oh so grown up with that fabric constraining her youthful body. Why, the beribboned fabric studded with whale bone whittled her waist to a mere seventeen inches giving her bragging rights for the rest of her days. Her second undervest arrived just before her wedding. In 1899, a young bride was not fully dressed without a ribbon embroidered corset beneath her chemise, petticoats, and gown. As her body began to blossom with her first child, the unforgiving bones pinched the flesh causing the sores that plagued Mary Ann all her life. Her little sister, Maudie and her husband's brother, Ray, were married almost a year after Mary Ann and Alden's ceremony. The youngers invited the olders to don their wedding fripperies again that they might share a wedding portrait. A five month pregnant Mary Ann was pinned and basted into her dress, and her discomfort showed in a face that looked as pinched as her waist. She took to stuffing bits of cotton, fabric, and soft tissue around those spots, anything to ease the chaffing. Of an evening getting ready for bed, when she loosed the lacings, a little shower of odds and ends would fall about her feet. When the shower became a storm, it was time to order a new pale peach corset.

When I was very little, Grandma was quick with a nursery rhyme to fit every occasion. She had memorized the rhymes at her father's knee, that she might speak proper English. I particularly remember the one about the little girl who had a little curl smack in the middle of her forehead. When I was an adolescent, the nursery rhymes ceased, but she was always ready with advice or stories of her own deeds and misdeeds to bring home her points. Remarkable insights were to be harvested from her reflections.

Ride a cock horse to Banberry Cross
To see a fine lady upon a fine horse.
With rings on her fingers and bells on her toes,
She will have music where ever she goes.

One

Carey Bound

My first rememberin' was comin' to Carey in an oxcart in 18 and 83. I was just five year and sometimes allowed to walk alongside the wagon with my Mama and our cow. My Dear Daddy would swoop me up front of his saddle so's I felt like the princess of the world looking out over all my land. To the clomp clomp of the horse hooves, he'd repeat nursery rhymes from his childhood until I knew 'em by heart. He told me if I practiced the rhymes I'd grow up speakin' proper. Ever' night and ever' morning, my Sweet Mama would milk our cow. She'd scoop a bit of the top milk, put it in a crock, and by the time we stopped our cart for the next night there would be a magical bit of butter for our biscuits. My little sister, Maudie, was three and bawled all the way. Time we come nigh to the plot we was homesteadin', she finally stopped her belly achin' as if she was t' home.

Nineteenth century Europe held few prospects for young families. Famine, fighting, and feudal land holdings pushed and persuaded the young people to pursue better lives. The Mormons with a plan to convert and increase their numbers offered passage to those who would join their church. The family of Mary Ann's father, James Ainsworth, hailed from England. Her mother's people came from Sweden, near Stockholm. Both families took passage in steerage from Southhampton in 1859. James, then seven years, and Maria, five, may have played together below decks on the voyage.

Upon their passage through Ellis Island, little Maria was informed that her name would henceforth be Mariah, the American version of her name. The five year old made up her mind on the spot that she was born Maria and would die Maria. No man in uniform who talked funny would change her name.

With further support from the church, the families crossed the new land and found themselves in Utah. Maria and James married in Brigham City, 1876. The newlyweds moved on to Sublett, in southern Idaho, where they farmed and produced two baby girls. Mary Ann was born the year of the Bannock Indian War, 1878. Maudie peeked out two years later.

Us Mormon families was leap froggin' all over south Ideeho lookin' for just the right spot to light.

Greener pastures were promised in the Carey Valley, so press on they did. Carey was about seventy miles as the crow flew from Sublett. With two small children, ox wagon, cow, horse, and assorted poultry the going was slow. There was no direct trail into the valley, so the little family had to follow the beaten path north and west, ferry across the Snake River, and head even further west before turning north and back east. They passed the occasional stone chimney standing sentinel over an abandoned homestead. The sad remains of a kitchen garden or a clump of forgotten posies suggested the woman of that sorry little house had tried to give it a go and had once called the place home. The little foursome threaded their way through the boulders polka dotting the pass. The journey had been close to a hundred miles when they finally laid eyes on the patchwork of farms that quilted Carey Valley.

After establishing his rights and marking his land, James built a temporary corral for the oxen, cow, and horse. He laughingly called himself a sodbuster, but he hoped someday to be a stockman and run cattle and sheep on his ranch. Mary Ann helped when she could and minded Little Maudie who was tethered to the oxcart. James fastened a kind of tent to the side of the cart for sleeping quarters and shade until he could build their first shelter. Maria made do. She cooked over an open fire in the yard and laundered their clothes in the nearby spring.

In time, James fashioned a home of unpeeled logs. He began with a big windowless room where Maria could cook in the fireplace. The family sat on rough hewn benches and slept on pallets. In time leantos were added as kitchen and bedrooms.

Any spare daylight found James grubbing out sagebrush, Maria at his side. It was important to clear their farm of *bloat brush*. If the livestock ate it, their bellies would swell near to popping and they would suffer an agonizing death. There could be no lolly gagging as they readied the soil for the plow. The survival of the family depended upon pulling crops from the land as soon as possible.

Of an evening, if he was not busy sewing a harness or mending a tool, James dandled his daughters on his knees, forever repeating the nursery rhymes he had learned in his own unschooled childhood. The girls learned their early lessons from Little Tommy Tucker and Miss Muffet, but a favorite was

> Trot trot to London
> Trot trot to Linn
> Watch out little girl
> Or you might fall in

at which point James spread his knees and the giggling girls fell through. Those were the special times.

One morning, while James was afield, Maria spotted two Indians as they walked up the path to the Ainsworth door. She knew of no problems in the territory, but the strangers scared the soup out of her. She shooed the girls onto a far corner pallet and gestured for Mary Ann to keep Maudie quiet. The frightened mother drew the latch string, quietly slid the bolt, and grabbed a butchering knife from the makeshift table. She stood silently by the door in the windowless room willing the strangers to go away. The men heard no one at home and left. Lord only knew what they wanted. Maria took a deep breath and moved to look after her girls. Mary Ann, in an effort to keep her baby sister from crying out, was just moments from smothering Maudie in the bedclothes.

While Maria labored in the field beside her husband, Mary Ann learned to start the dinner, bake the biscuits, and do the family laundry. One morning, while snapping the wrinkles out of a wet shirt to hang on the drying line, she chipped her front tooth on a button. Mama told her to praise God she had not put out an eye and be more careful next time. The tooth discolored, she was teased at Sunday school, and the embarrassed little girl learned to smile ever after with her mouth closed.

James discovered a bee tree on his land. Sugar was dear so they were always after the sweetening. He and Mary Ann would collect honey of an evening because it was cooler at dusk and the bees would be less active and less apt to sting the hive robbers. Upon their return home, it was Mary Ann's job to strain the sweet nectar so as not to spread bees knees on their breakfast biscuits.

About three years after their move to Carey, James had his son. They called him Baby Boy Albert. Maria suffered from milk fever so she was unable to put the child to nurse. James contrived a teat from a leather glove finger and secured it to a flask which he filled with cow milk. As James continued to prove up his homestead, the girls learned to feed and care for their baby brother and accomplish most of the household chores. Albert failed to thrive, and they buried him when he was just eighteen months old. Weakened by the pregnancy, the fever, and the loss of her child it seemed Maria would never be quite the same. Nine year old Mary Ann blamed and punished herself for Albert's death. She never quite set aside the grief.

When Maria finally saw a doctor, he shook his head and said, "No more babies, Mrs. Ainsworth." His pronouncement was the beginning of the end for the little family. Over the next few years James worked diligently to finish the house, construct out buildings, and make the little farm productive. His daughters shouldered many of the chores both inside and out. There was no dawdling for Mary Ann and Maudie. They were pressed to go to school where they excelled in recitation and handwriting. Along with their books they carried their shoes to school, weather permitting, saving them for Sunday best.

One spring, as the daffodils colored the side yard and showed their slender throats, James packed his bags and took himself off for California. While Maria was saddened but not surprised, the girls were devastated. James, determined to make his fortune, promised to send his three girls money every month. He did.

Maria, thereafter, was called *the widder woman*. With help from the girls she continued to make do on their little farm. Mary Ann made the garden her very own while Maudie tended to their animals. Hired hands pitched in with the heavy plowing and harvesting of the potatoes and animal fodder. Maria bought fabric and thread with the first money she received from her estranged husband, and she advertised herself as a seamstress. She sewed deep into the night with a kerosene lantern to light her work space. She saved a little from each month's allotment and in time she had put by enough to order a catalogue sewing machine. The three girls loved and protected each other, but much of the fun and laughter was gone from their lives. Maria never looked to find another partner, nor did James.

When times were tough we always had spuds.

Maria's Spud Soup

6 slices	bacon, chopped in small pieces
2	onions, diced
3-4	potatoes, peeled and diced
2	stalks celery, diced
2	carrots, diced
1 cup	corn
	water
1 teaspoon	salt
½ teaspoon	pepper
½ teaspoon	dry sage, rubbed between palms of hands over soup
¼ cup	butter

In a Dutch oven or soup pot, brown the bacon. Add the onions and cook until translucent. Add the potatoes, celery, carrots, and corn. Add water just to cover. Simmer for 45 minutes to an hour. Add salt, pepper, and sage. Finish with butter.

If there were milk or cream available, a cup or so would be added just before serving.

Serves 6.

Maria's Spuds and Butter

¼ cup	butter
3-4	large baking potatoes, peeled, sliced in 1/8 inch slices
	salt
	pepper
	dry sage

Preheat oven to 450°.

In a large cast iron fry pan or ovenproof skillet, melt butter. Leave one tablespoon butter in the pan and set aside three tablespoonsful.

Make a single layer of potatoes over bottom of pan. Salt and pepper, rub sage between palms of hands, and sprinkle with about two teaspoonsful of the butter. Repeat layers four or five times, ending with the remaining butter. Pack down. Cover.

Bake at 450° 20 minutes. Uncover and bake 25 minutes.

Loosen edges, invert on a serving plate. Dust with sage. Slice into wedges.

Serves 6 to 8 servings.

Wee Willie Winkie runs through the town
Upstairs and downstairs in his nightgown.
Rapping at the window, crying through the lock,
"Are the children in their beds? Now it's eight o'clock."

Two

Hide and Seek

I learned most of Mother Mary's story from her son, my Dear Alden. I'm suspectin' it grieved her too much to think on it, let alone tell it. I can't even imagine the heart hurt that must come to a wife put aside or replaced. Mary's marriage to John was broke beyond repair. The Mormons in those days thought they was doin' right by the Church, but they sure wasn't doin' right by first wives and their children. The elders claimed there was all these extree women needin' homes after their men died trekkin' to Utah. Mary didn't take a shine to this notion 't all.

The pushcart Mormons headed west to a promise with a prayer. Unable to afford teams of oxen to pull the heavy wagons, they cut their loads, built their carts, and pushed or pulled them all the way to Utah's valleys. With faith and years of toil they sculpted their land of milk and honey.

With so many of their numbers lost to attack, hunger, exhaustion, and illness along the way, there was an implied assumption that there were more females than males upon reaching their destination. Church elders proposed that those men able to support more than one family should take on the responsibility of another wife. Rumor had it those same churchmen determined a man needed at least three wives if he was to be heaven bound.

Mary first noticed the changes in her husband not long after Little Ray was born. John Ivie became a church elder. He started dressing a little smarter, waxing his mustache, stepping a little higher, and eyeing the single and widowed young women at church doings. John would take a second bride. Now, a first wife was to give permission for her husband to take another wife. Without a murmur or a whine, Mary decided she would have none of it. Although married to a pious man, having borne three daughters and two sons, she simply would not have another woman in her house.

She began to make her plans and collect her few possessions. Mary packed some cooking utensils and quietly accumulated provisions and the few trinkets she had managed to keep on their westward trek. Wrapped and tied in clothing for herself and her son Aldey, along with hoarded food to sustain them on their journey, she hid the necessaries beneath some hay in the barn.

She set her plans to escape by night. She knew she could not take her baby son, barely three years old. Little Ray would be startled, would cry out, and give them away. Oh how she would miss the smile that crinkled Ray's dear little eyes almost to disappearing when he laughed. She would rely on her husband and older daughters to give him proper nurturing and love. She would collect Little Ray as soon as she could, when he was old enough to understand.

With eight year old Aldey she plotted the game. She told him they would be playing hide and seek with his father. Now his mother was always up for frolic, but the little boy found it difficult to imagine his stern father, quick with a razor strop, would play any game. That very evening after supper, Mary went to the barn ostensibly to leave scraps for the barn kittens. While there, she harnessed a horse and tied their few belongings and food to the saddle. She told her son the game would begin that night. Aldey should go to bed fully clothed and she would rouse him when it was time to play. Awakening and hushing him, they headed for the barn by moonlight, rendered dim by wispy clouds, and quietly walked their provisioned mount in the direction of the road. Done with the farm, they high tailed it for the Idaho border. Mary expected they would be followed. As it turned out, they were not. No one considered a disgruntled wife an asset.

Aldey did enjoy a good game, but a little voice in his head told him to pay attention to his surroundings, just in case the romp went awry. He attended to the road and landmarks all the way north. The eight year old took in the unfamiliar landscape, held his breath, and closed his eyes as if to capture a tintype he could hold in his mind's eye forever. Picture upon picture, the tiniest turn in the trail he committed to memory. He was uncertain as to why it all seemed so important.

Traveling by day, camping by night, the twosome ate biscuits and salt ham, always careful to top off the water in their flask. With few words, Mary told Aldey why they were on the trail, and he heard the catch in her throat when she spoke of leaving Little Ray behind. Aldey's questions went unasked out of loyalty to his mother, and many years passed before he fully understood.

The pair had almost run through the stale biscuits when they came upon Carey Valley in southern Idaho. A lush landscape, unlike the desolate valleys yet to be irrigated in Utah, Carey promised twice the crops with half the perspiration.

Mother and son settled into an abandoned cabin, more of a shed, on the homestead of a shirttail relative. With just a few coins in their keeping, they cobbled together a little life for themselves. Mary took in laundry and mending while Aldey went to school and hired himself out to perform odd chores on the surrounding farms.

Now, Mary considered herself a grass widow, a woman who had been replaced or set aside while her husband continued to live above the grass. In time, she dropped the *grass* and let it be known she was simply a widow.

After a time, an old bachelor came courting. Lyman Peters lived on a neighboring farm and made Mary's acquaintance when he brought by his coveralls and shirts in need of a good lathering and a button or two. A kind man, he took time with Aldey and taught the young one to whittle and to play mumblety peg with his pearl handled jackknife. Mr. Peters was happy to share a few fishing tricks. Smitten with Mary, the old gentleman took himself home and added a leanto bedroom, fresh paint, and furniture, the better to receive the woman and her son.

Mary took him to husband and moved Aldey and their few possessions to Mr. Peter's farm. She kept her washtubs and clotheslines full and her needle at the ready. She used her sugar bowl money to keep Aldey in overalls and boots and books. Occasionally she bought a length of dress fabric for herself. A few extra pennies meant a chew of tobacco for her good man. She happily set out roots like an old potato and never moved again.

Mother Mary, in the German way, salted away her cabbage and put a huge barrel of sauerkraut to rest every October, just after spud harvest. It was ready in about eight weeks in time for winter cooking. It was the dependable vegetable that kept the family through the winter.

Mother Mary's Pork and 'Kraut

4-5	large pork chops or meaty spare ribs
1 tablespoon	bacon grease, butter, or oil for browning
4 cups	sauerkraut
2-3	peeled, chopped apples
½ cup	sugar
1 tablespoons	molasses or brown sugar
¼ teaspoon	salt
¼ teaspoon	pepper

Brown meat in a little oil in a pot. Add the remaining ingredients and simmer 3 hours. Check seasonings before serving.

Mother Mary sometimes used chopped dried apples and added extree sauerkraut juice.

Serves 4 or 5.

Some said Mother Mary was such a good cook she had folks a settin' at her table before she even rang the dinner bell.

Mother Mary's Sugar Sweet Pie

1 ½ cups	flour
1 cup	brown sugar
½ teaspoon	cinnamon
½ teaspoon	nutmeg
¼ cup	butter
½ teaspoon	baking soda
¾ cup	lukewarm water
½ cup	molasses

Preheat oven to 350°.

Prepare a one crust pastry, lard or butter.

Combine flour, brown sugar, cinnamon, nutmeg, and butter until the mixture is crumbly.

In another bowl, combine baking soda with warm water and molasses. Pour the liquid into the pie shell and sprinkle with the crumbled mixture.

Bake at 350° for 45 minutes or until pie is set. The pie will set some as it cools.

In the Pennsylvania Dutch tradition, Mother Mary served seven sweets and seven sours.

Rain, rain go away
Come again another day.
Little Johnny wants to play.

Three

A Friend In Need

We farm folk and ranchers in Ideeho were not always the most welcoming to the Basques. They roamed the grassy places with their sheep, their dogs, and their funny little wagons. We suspicioned their language, their food, and their wandering ways.

It was good to be out and about. Aldey's mother had packed a lunch of breakfast leftovers. He had a school free afternoon and a plan to bring home a mess of trout for dinner. Mounted bareback on his pony and enjoying the warm afternoon, he dismissed the humidity as the coolish air whisked by his face. Riding south across the wash and up the draw in the direction of his favorite fishing hole, he failed to notice the dark clouds accumulating at his back.

He found himself a comfortable perch by the stream in the shade of his beloved aspen, and he listened to the serenade of their leaves as he paid out his fishing line. Their music became louder as the leaves danced beneath the darkening sky. Then came lightning followed by fierce clatter. He gathered his gear and headed for home as he knew the wash could soon fill and halt his way.

He approached the gorge and his fears were justified. The dry stream bed surged with new run off. Buffeted by the wind and rain, he rode beside the overflow, seeking a safe place to cross. There was no crossing to be found. Just ahead on a rise he spotted a Basque sheep wagon. Now, he had heard some stories about those peculiar folk and their strange ways. Cold and wet to the skin as he was, the tales did not seem much to matter. Shelter would be good, and perhaps something warm to drink. Aldey made his way to the little wagon through the downpour.

Greeted and welcomed, an old Basque gentleman threw a blanket over the boy's thin shoulders and drew him inside by the warm cook stove. Mr. Ibnez introduced himself. His English was as broken as his teeth, but his eyes were warm. They secured Aldey's pony in the near shelter of the wagon. Haltingly, the older man asked the boy's name as he poured a warm fruit laden drink laced with spices for the chilled youngster. In all the fuss and flurry, Aldey had almost forgotten how hungry he was. As Aldey described the location of his home and his reason for having crossed the ravine, the old gentleman spread some sheep milk cheese on a hunk of crusty bread with the back of a spoon. Between the soothing and filling bites, the two continued to chat by fire glow. A pot of thick lamb stew, heavy with spice, had been simmering on the little stove. The two shared dinner. Seasoned with garlic and peppers, the meat tasted foreign on Aldey's tongue.

As the storm continued, Mr. Ibnez arranged a comfy pallet for Aldey. Warm and quiet, listening to the staccato of rain falling on the roof, the boy watched the little Basque mix and stir dough by candle and stove light. Tired as he was, Aldey was not quite ready for sleep. He was full of questions, and the kind old man satisfied the boy with answers.

Mr. Ibnez fed the sourdough. Sourdough, he explained, was alive. It started as a sponge of flour and water, yeast and sugar. If a cook treated it well and handled it correctly, the dough could last forever. Like a child it must be kept warm, fed, allowed to rest, and be well attended. On the trail the cook often took the crock to bed to keep it warm, but the sourdough would be warm enough in the wagon. The old man added warm water, flour, yeast and a little sugar to the crock. He gave it a good stir and a talking to. He divided off about half of the dough and placed it another bowl which he covered. That would be tomorrow morning's pancakes and bread. The remainder was left in the crock. He gave it a firm pat, and put it to bed. Then he took himself to bed.

Sleep finally found Aldey. He awoke next morning to more rain, warm milk, and the most delicious pancakes he had ever tasted. Aldey watched as his new friend separated last night's bowl into two smaller bowls. To one he added sheep milk, an egg, and flour, finally ladling the batter onto a sizzling griddle. A thick syrup of sweetened choke cherries ran over and down the sides of the fluffy hot cakes.

After breakfast, the old man added ingredients to the second bowl, covered it, and left the bread to rise by the stove. He and Aldey headed out to survey the damage of the previous night. Satisfied that his faithful dog had gathered in the sheep, the old man and youngster made their way in the direction of the wash. Still high water, Aldey would wait until later in the day to make his way home.

As the morning progressed, so did the friendship. Mr. Ibnez and Aldey settled in and shared their stories. The man had come from the Old Country in the Pyrenees with his lady and a man child. They had first gone to Argentina, made a little money, had a girl baby, and decided to move on to the United States. His wife died and was buried at sea. Upon his arrival in New York, the man had labored to keep his children sheltered and fed. His daughter married and his son joined the army. Free of his parental responsibilities, Mr. Ibnez made his way west. The open lands of Idaho revived memories of his youth in the Basque countryside. He had not enough savings to buy land, so he bought three sheep and built himself a wagon in the old way. A stray dog joined his little household, and in time his herd increased. He had come full circle and he embraced the life of a wanderer.

Aldey, for all his almost thirteen years, had a sad little story to share. He relived his mother's hide and seek game of four years ago and told of their flight to Carey. Aldey conjured up the face of his moist eyed mother when she spoke of her lost child, Little Ray, the left behind brother in Utah.

The thoughtful old Basque interrupted the reverie of the youngster with a challenge. "Your little brother be feeling like a bummer lamb, not wanted by his mother. You must go rescue that little brother, let him know the truth. Bring him home to his mama."

Now, Aldey was full of doubt, but the kind old gentleman reminded him that little brother Ray was the almost eight, about the same age Aldey had been when he and his mother had fled north. "It be time you show that little brother how the game is played."

Aldey stayed long enough to be taught more secrets about the sourdough. He learned to make the bread he had so relished at the evening meal. He listened carefully as Mr. Ibnez explained how he might also make biscuits from the starter, remembering always to replenish, nurture, talk to it, and keep it warm. Aldey took his leave that afternoon with many thanks and a small crock of sourdough starter under his arm.

Mindful of the old gentleman's words of encouragement, Aldey picked his way home through the slippery stones and mud. Full of plans to rescue Little Ray, he decided it was too early to share them with his mother and stepfather. He would think on it.

Over the years, Dear Alden made many a sourdough recipe from the starter Mr. Ibnez had gifted him so long before. The starter was shared with family and friends. It was the very idee of time and love.

Ibnez Sourdough Starter

1 package	dry yeast
½ cup	warm water
2 cups	flour
2 cups	warm water
1 tablespoon	sugar

Soften the yeast in the ½ cup warm water. Add the remaining ingredients and combine until smooth. Place in a large bowl, cover with a plate, and allow to stand at room temperature three to five days, stirring two to three times daily. Refrigerate. Bring it back to room temperature when you are ready to use it.

Put about a cup of this dough in a covered crock (this is your original sourdough starter) and use the remainder for your chosen recipe.

Note: If you are not going to use the starter for awhile, add 1 teaspoon sugar every ten days or so and keep refrigerated. As I don't bake often, I freeze the crock. The day before I plan to use the sourdough, I let the crock come to room temperature and refresh it with a bit of warm water, a sprinkle of yeast, and a sprinkle of sugar.

The Night Before

or

Sharing the Starter

1 cup (about)	sourdough starter
2 cups	warm water
2 cups	flour
1 teaspoon	dry yeast

The night before you are planning to bake, or if you wish to share your starter, put the sourdough starter, the warm water, flour, and yeast in a mixing bowl. Combine. Put one cup of the starter back in the crock. This will be your "original" starter. Leave the crock and the covered bowl at room temperature overnight.

Ibnez Sourdough Bread and Rolls

1 package	dry yeast
¼ cup	warm water
2 tablespoons	sugar
1 teaspoon	salt
2 tablespoons	melted butter or oil
4 cups	flour, more or less
¼ teaspoon	soda

Soften the yeast in water and add to sourdough sponge in the bowl along with the sugar, salt, and shortening. Add about half of the flour and mix well. Cover and allow to rise about an hour. Add soda to remaining flour and mix into sponge. Turn onto a floured surface and knead. Cover and let rise once again. Shape into loaves or rolls. Let rise again.

Preheat oven to 375°.
Bake at   375° about 50 minutes for loaves or about 30 minutes for rolls.

Ibnez Basque Bread and Garlic Soup

¼ cup	olive oil
4-6 cloves	garlic, peeled and sliced
½ teaspoon	red pepper flakes, crushed
2 cups	bread, dried and cubed
4 cups	chicken broth
2	eggs

Heat oil in a Dutch pot or soup pot. Add garlic and simmer until golden. Crush pepper between palms of hands over the garlic.

Reserve a few cubes of bread to garnish the soup, then toss the remainder with the oil, garlic, and red pepper. Add broth, cover, and simmer 20 minutes.

Beat eggs in a small bowl. Combine about one half cup of the hot broth with the eggs. Put the egg and soup mixture back to the soup pot and let soup thicken.

Serves 4-5.

Ibnez Basque Lamb Stew

¼ cup	olive oil
2 tablespoons	flour
½ teaspoon	salt
2 pounds	lamb cut into 1 inch pieces
2-3 cloves	garlic
1	onion, chopped
1 teaspoon	red pepper flakes, crushed
3-4	potatoes, peeled and cut in 1 inch pieces
4 cups	broth, lamb or beef or chicken
2 tablespoons	cornstarch
¼ cup	water

In a Dutch oven or large pot, heat oil. Combine flour and salt to dredge lamb pieces. Brown the lamb in the oil. Remove the meat and set it aside. Add the garlic and onion to remaining oil. Cook until onion is translucent. Crush pepper between palms of hands over onions and garlic. Add back browned lamb, potatoes, and broth.

Cover and simmer one to one and a half hours.

In a small bowl, combine cornstarch and water and add to the stew to thicken the gravy.

Serves 6 to 8.

Carrots, celery, corn, squash, tomatoes may be added with the potatoes.

When I was a bachelor
I lived all by myself
And all the bread and cheese I got
I laid upon my shelf.

Four

Kidnap

Now, along with sourdough recipes, old Mr. Ibnez had put some idees into Alden's head. Fetching his little brother from Utah would please their Mama and complete their little family. Can you just imagine a thirteen year old boy headin' off to Lord knows what to kidnap his eight year old brother? Some folks said he was plum foolish. I think he was plum brave.

Long and hard Aldey thought out how he would pursue his plan. He prayed his little brother had not fallen heir to the razor strop whippings which Aldey escaped five years before. Little Ray would not know his older brother, would not simply come away with him. Aldey would take a small tintype of their mother and stories to share of their life in Idaho. Now that sourdough was his good friend, the boys would not be hungry on the trail. He borrowed dried apples and bacon from his mother's larder. He rounded up a Dutch oven and he located a jug to hold his water supply.

As he quietly gathered his provisions, Aldey decided he would also borrow his stepfather's horse, that it might carry the two boys north. Using his best penmanship, he wrote a note explaining that he needed the larger horse and that he would return in time with a nice surprise for his mother. He then headed south for Utah. Had he told the folks his plan, they would not have let him go.

Aldey knew why he had paid such careful attention on that trek north years before. There was not a turn in the road or a landmark he did not recognize although the passage of time and folk left the trail deeper and wider. Traveling by day, he stopped at night to rest and to divide and refresh his sourdough. Trained to do his bidding, it fermented and rose on the journey.He enjoyed biscuits and pancakes all along his route.

Aldey set a little camp for himself, up the draw just east of his father's farm. A stream provided water and fish while he waited to make his move. He knew the lay of the farm and he eventually spotted little brother going about his chores. Aldey made himself known to Little Ray but kept their kinship to himself. As trust built between the two, Aldey invited the younger boy to his secluded campsite. Over a little lunch of biscuits and trout, Aldey produced the tintype of their mother and explained that he had come to Utah to take his brother home. The lady in the picture looked familiar. On the edge of his remembrance, Ray could almost hear a nice lady singing to him. The little boy had been told his mother was dead, and he had no knowledge of a brother. Aldey's tale of their flight five years before plucked at his younger brother's heart strings. Little Ray finally understood why father and stepmother seemed to have no time or affection for him. Ray had not smiled in a very long time. Although more children had come along, Little Ray's childhood had been a lonely one.

It did not take much convincing for the eight year old to join his big brother. As it turned out, they did not have to play the game of hide and seek. Ray flew home and fetched his few possessions thrown into an frayed flour sack. The boys quickly dissolved the campsite and lit out for Idaho that very afternoon. They rode all that night by moonlight and most of the next day. They sipped water, chewed on stale biscuits, and sucked dried apples.

The second night, they stopped to rest. Aldey showed off one of his sourdough tricks and the boys smacked their way through dinner. They shared their blankets with the sourdough starter, as Mr. Ibnez had told Aldey, and they talked late into the night about their Mama and her kind Mr.Peters. Aldey recollected Little Ray showed no signs of being homesick for Utah or his Daddy. The journey was a happy one. Little Ray felt safe and secure and well fed in his brother's keeping, and he happily clung to Aldey's back and nodded off now and again as they headed north.

A surprise indeed clambered up the road, two boys astride the big borrowed mount. There was great rejoicing, and the story of kidnap soon spread among the neighbors. Mary delighted in having her young son, crinkly eyed smile, and all. They had lots of catching up to do. She was forever grateful to her eldest. Gathering her boys about her, she began to sing again. Aldey took his grown up name, Alden, and Mr. Peters handily added another leanto so the boys would have their own space to bond and thrive.

On the trail, Alden made his sourdough biscuits and concocted a little supper of vittles he carried when he went to fetch his little brother. Over the years, he perfected this recipe adding a little here and there. It was Dear Alden's Supper.

Alden's Sourdough Biscuits

1 cup	sourdough starter
1 cup	warm water
1 cup	flour
1 teaspoon	dry yeast

The night before you are planning to bake, put your starter, the warm water, flour, and yeast in a mixing bowl. Mix and put one cup of the starter back in the crock. Leave the crock and the covered bowl at room temperature overnight.

1 1/3 cups	flour
2 teaspoon	baking powder
½ teaspoon	soda
½ teaspoon	salt
1/3 cup	shortening
1 cup	sourdough starter
2 tablespoons	melted butter

Preheat oven to 425°.
Combine flour, baking powder, soda, salt, and shortening with a pastry blender. Add sourdough starter. Stir just enough to moisten mixture. Turn onto a floured surface. Roll dough to about ½ inch thick and cut in two inch rounds. Place on a greased cookie sheet. Brush with melted butter. Allow to rise about one hour or until doubled.
Bake at 425° 15 minutes or until golden.
Makes about 12 biscuits.

Alden's Dutch Oven Bacon and Apples

2 cups	dried apples, sliced or chunked
2 cups	boiling water
½ pound	bacon chopped in ¼ inch pieces
½	onion, chopped
	pepper

Reconstitute apples in boiling water. Drain and set aside.

Fry bacon in a Dutch oven or fry pan until almost crisp. Stir in onion and continue to cook until onion is translucent. Stir in apples. Cover and let simmer about ten minutes.

Serve with biscuits.

Fresh sliced apples may be used in place of the dried apples.

Serves 2-3.

Bless you, bless you, Burnie Bee
And tell me when my wedding be.
If it be tomorrow day
Take your wings and fly away.
Fly to the east, fly to the west.
Fly to him I love the best.

Five

Weddings

Now, I was considered a looker with my dark eyes and seventeen inch waist. My mama wouldn't let me wear any lip rouge, but I knew to bite my lips and pinch my cheeks red. And I was allowed a dab of vanilla behind each ear. I had a few of them Carey boys a buzzin' like bees for the honey. Then along come Alden.

We was at a church picnic, and I was a lollygaggin' in the wagon, just waitin' for him to come and help me down. As he hefted me, I was hopin' he'd be noticin' my tiny waist. I blushed at the thought of him feelin' the whale bone of my corset through my summer calico, wishing he couldn't and glad that he would. 'Twasn't long after Dear Alden came a courtin' and we took to picnickin' and camping 'round about Carey. Now we was always chaperoned by Sweet Sister Maudie or Alden's brother, Ray. We was young, we was healthy, and we was in love. We set a wedding date for August.

My but weren't we itchin'? 'fore long, we was disappearing and scratchin' where we itched. Sometimes both Maudie and Ray would chaperone, and 'twasn't long before they decided they was in love. Glory be, those camping trips and picnics. I wonder still if the neighbors talked about those Ainsworth girls and those Ivie boys.

My Sweet Mama had purchased a length of silk and was fashionin' my weddin' gown. Not so very long before the weddin', she asked if she was goin' to have to let out the waist. I was 'shamed that she'd figgered out the goin's on, and I didn't want to embarrass my mama none. We were just plain lucky me and Alden wasn't caught with a baby.

Within the week after Alden asked for Mary Ann's hand in marriage, Maria set to writing a letter to her gallavanting husband in California. Now, most folks wore their Sunday best for *big doin's* like weddings, but Maria had her heart set on decking out her eldest daughter in the manner she had always wanted to dress her girls. By return mail, she received a substantial money order and, with Mary Ann, selected the fabric for the wedding gown. They thumbed through catalogues, looking for just the right pattern to copy. Mary Ann, ever proud of her tiny waist, finally settled upon a pattern that would accentuate her best feature. Maria cut the fabric. She set aside usable scraps with plans to make embroidered pillows for the babies Mary Ann and Alden would have. She surmised she had enough leftovers for at least four pillows. She basted, fit, and finally sewed the dainty dress stitches by hand. She covered tiny buttons with silk and crocheted the button loops in perfectly matched thread. The dress was of silk, fine as gossamer. This sheer fabric would also serve as Mary Ann's veil. The lining, by necessity, was of a heavier ivory silk which would render the dress terribly warm come August. Maria worked on the layers of gown and designed a traveling costume for Mary Ann's honeymoon trip. These she managed between other sewing projects that kept food on the table.

Mary Ann, along with her mother and sister, sewed up a storm hemming sheets and towels and making curtains for the one tiny window in the little cabin she and Alden would call home. Mary Ann had practiced stitching ampersands for years and had in fact stitched *& Mary Ann* on many of her linens. At long last she was able to finish the embroidery, *Alden & Mary Ann*. She considered herself very organized. Their little nest was perched on a corner of the property owned by Lyman Peters and

34

Alden's mother. Just one room, they would eventually add a kitchen and a bedroom leanto for themselves. As the children came along, they would add yet another bedroom on the north side.

The wedding was simple, a cake and punch affair. Then the family returned to Maria's house and table for a little celebratory lunch. After the meal, Ray announced that he and Maudie would marry the following August. Far from surprised, Maria smiled and nodded. It crossed her mind that close as the girls were, they could share the gown Mary Ann had worn that day. Maria would have to let out the waist a trifle and perhaps do a few repairs to the button loops, but a good deal of time and money would be saved. As it happened, the roving photographer had not come through the territory to immortalize Mary Ann and Alden's marriage, so just as Ray finished his announcement, Maudie had one of her own. She had decided that since her sister and new brother-in-law had no photograph of their big day, they would join together the following August in all their wedding finery and have a formal portrait taken together, the four of them. So much for the shared gown idea. Maria wrote her husband the next week with the plans and a request for more wedding money. Glory be! Girls were expensive.

After our wedding, we went home to my Sweet Mama's house for a little lunch. She served up my favorite cake for our wedding.

Maria's Carrot Cake with Milk Frosting

2 cups	flour
2 teaspoons	soda
½ teaspoon	salt
2 teaspoons	cinnamon
1 teaspoon	nutmeg
1 cup	applesauce
½ cup	buttermilk
3	eggs
1 ¾ cups	sugar
2 tablespoons	butter, melted and cooled
3 cups	grated or finely chopped carrots
½ cup	raisins
½ cup	walnuts, chopped

Preheat oven to 375°.
Grease and flour a 13x9 inch baking pan or two 8" round cake pans.

Combine flour, soda, salt, cinnamon, and nutmeg. In a larger bowl, combine applesauce, buttermilk, eggs, sugar and melted butter. Fold in dry ingredients, then fold in grated carrots, raisins, and walnuts. Pour into greased and floured pan or pans. Drop pan about three inches onto counter to bring air bubbles to the top.

Bake at 375° 30-35 minutes or until done in the center for 13x9" pan or 25-30 minutes for eight inch pans. Cool completely before frosting.

Serves 10 to 12.

Milk Frosting

1 cup	milk
3 tablespoons	flour
1 cup	butter, at room temperature
1 cup	sugar
pinch	salt
2 teaspoons	vanilla

Combine milk and flour. Cook in a small saucepan, stirring constantly, until mixture thickens. Cool.

While the white sauce is cooling, in a bowl combine the butter, sugar, salt, and vanilla.

Add the cooled white sauce and beat until you can't feel the sugar granules on your tongue. Frost the cake.
Makes enough to frost a two layer cake.

Peter Peter pumpkin eater,
Had a wife and couldn't keep her.
Put her in a pumpkin shell
And there he kept her very well.

Six

Honeymoon

Alden truly tried to enjoy the day's wedding festivities. He smiled until his jaw hurt. But his mind leaped to honeymoon time, on the way to conquer a mountain.

Not far from Carey grew Hyndman Peak which was thought to be the highest in the state at 12,078 feet. Now, Alden had been hankering to climb that mountain for years. Mary Ann was game, so he gave her a pair of proper walking boots as a wedding present, made his plans, and collected the bedrolls and camping equipment they would need. Caught up in the flurry of excitement and wishing to share their happiness, they invited Alden's older sister Ida, his brother Ray and half brother Arthur, and three friends to accompany them on their trek. Mary Ann amazed herself that she had agreed to honeymoon on the mountain.

As reported in the Wood River Journal, the party of eight "started from East Fork of the Little Wood River on a trip into the Idaho forest with full intention of visiting Hyndman's peak before returning home. Our means of conveyance was a wagon for a distance of eight miles, when we were compelled to use pack animals for six more miles and, incidentally to walk which took us to the base of the big mountain. The next day, while scanning the hill and planning an ascent, one of our party shot a large cinnamon bear."

The morning of the big climb, they awoke to the quiet of the little aspen wood where they had made their base camp. Soon the clatter of cooking mixed with birdsong. Campers all, they slept in their clothes. Dressing amounted to relief behind a bush, a straigtening of their garments, and a quick wash of hands and faces. The women fussed a little with their hair. They consumed a bountiful breakfast of Dutch oven spuds, onions, and eggs, and sourdough hot cakes which Alden had started the night before. The girls rustled up a picnic lunch and filled flasks with spring water to take along.

Clouds began to accumulate around the peak with bone chilling damp while at their base camp below it was just another sweltering August day. Mary Ann clutched at her jacket, wishing she had worn just one more layer. Her skirts and petticoats hobbled her every move. That she might move more freely on their final ascent, she hiked up her skirts. She pulled the fabric up between her legs and fastened it with a ribbon from her bodice. She could actually see the newly scuffed boots on her tiny feet inching forward up the grade. She struggled to find purchase on the slippery incline, she balanced and clung to the rocks on her left and felt the new wide gold band beneath her glove. Alden grasped her elbow to steady her. She knew she must concentrate on every footstep, but her mind took little vacations and filled with images of her wedding day, her wedding night, the sons she would give her Dear Alden. With the altitude her lungs longed for more oxygen, and her breath came in little raggedy gasps. As she stumbled up the rocky way and Alden steadied her, she was overwhelmed with mixed feelings. She relished the adventure of the climb to the peak with her young and strong husband as guide, yet part of her wished they had stayed home in Carey and played house.

The clouds disappeared as if on cue when they reached the summit. Footsore and laughing in triumph, they shared their picnic lunch and passed a flask of water. They sat a spell, her hand in his, and surveyed their kingdom below. Alden showed her the world from that mountain top. He pointed to an area south and east, Carey. There they would live and rear their family. Little did Mary Ann know that as she scanned the north and east, she was looking upon what would become her second home. To the south and west would be her last home and final resting place.

The newspaper report continued, "The next day we packed a fine picnic, readied a flagpole, and began our climb at 9 a.m. sharp. The day was hot, the climb precipitous, but I must say I never saw two young ladies with so much pluck or nerve. We reached the summit at five o'clock in the evening, and the scenery was grand and beautiful. We built a large mound of rocks, placed our names in a crevice on the top, and flew from it the flag we had brought -an American flag- to fly so long as it will. The trip up took eight hours, the descent three, and we rested at the base for a couple of days before returning home, knowing that we were the very first ever to get to the top of that 12,000 foot high Idaho mountain."

Some years later, Mary Ann learned that Mount Hyndman was not the highest point in Idaho. Borah Peak, to the north, was the taller by 584 feet. Mary Ann wistfully watched and measured that grand mountain and imagined her ascent. She climbed it only in her dreams.

Sourdough Hot Cakes

1 cup	sourdough starter
2 cups	warm water
3 cups	flour
1 teaspoon	dry yeast

The night before you are planning to make hot cakes, put your starter, warm water, flour, and yeast in a mixing bowl. Mix and put one cup of the starter back in the crock. Leave the crock and the covered bowl at room temperature overnight.

2	eggs
1 teaspoon	salt
2 teaspoons	baking powder
3 tablespoons	sugar
3 tablespoons	oil

To the sourdough mixture in the bowl, add eggs, salt, baking powder, sugar, and oil. If mixture seems too runny, add a little more flour. Stir only enough to combine and try not to deflate the sourdough bubbles. Ladle and fry on a hot griddle.

Makes 12 or so, depending on size of hot cakes.

Alden's Dutch Oven Beans

1 pound	dry navy or white beans
	water to cover
¼ pound	bacon or salt pork, cut in 1/2 inch pieces
1	large onion, sliced or diced
1/3 cup	molasses
1/3 cup	vinegar
1/3 cup	sugar or brown sugar
1 teaspoon	dry mustard
1 teaspoon	cinnamon
½ teaspoon	salt
½ teaspoon	pepper

Cover beans with water and allow to soak ten hours or overnight.

Drain.

In a Dutch oven, fry bacon or salt pork. When it is almost crisp, add the onion and cook until translucent. Stir in the molasses, vinegar, sugar, dry mustard, cinnamon, salt, pepper, and beans.

Cover and allow to simmer on the stove or fireside for several hours.

Serves 6-8.

Daffy-down-dilly has come to town
In a yellow petticoat and a green gown.

Seven

Playing House

*Dear Alden came to dinner with a big smile and a surprise
for me. He had fashioned a darning egg, carvin' and smoothin'
the wood just so. Now I had never learned to darn so very good,
leavin' that to my Dear Mama. Truth be told I was still runnin'
all my mendin' up to her. I'm guessin' Alden thought it was time
for me to be learnin' to make do for our little family.*

Mary Ann had cooked and cleaned and homekept for some
years before Alden marched into her life. She knew to garden, to
harvest, to put by. She blamed it on her new stove when she
somehow managed to burn the very first dinner she prepared in
their new home. She fanned the door in an effort to clear the
room of the smokey smell. With practice, the aroma of dinner
cooking was welcomed in the big room, except for the days she
cooked cabbage. In the afternoons Mary Ann trotted around her
home and garden like a frisky pony as she made sure everything
was just so for Dear Alden. Hearth was home.

Her husband built a sturdy bed and a wooden rocker she
could use in her big room or drag to the front porch to sit a spell.
Alden pictured his bride rocking their first son in that chair. He
also fashioned two high backed shelter benches, reminiscent of
the cupboard beds of Scandinavia, which Mary Ann warmed and
softened with the comfort of crazy quilts she, her Mama, and
sister had stitched. The furniture could be scooted by the fire or
moved to the window light or placed at the table. Shelves for
supplies, some hooks for their clothing, and a workbench
completed their little nest. The chamber pot fit neatly under the
bed so mostly Mary Ann didn't have to think about it.

The wooden floor was easier to keep clean than the dirt floor Mary Ann's family had when she was a child. She swept it everyday and mopped it twice a week. Those first months she took pride in the cooking and the homekeeping. Winter found her capturing Alden's frozen underdrawers where they shivered on the clothesline. She brought them inside to thaw by the fire. As days warmed and spring was in the air, she itched to get on with her garden and to magic up the shoots which would provide their food.

She put in raspberries and planted fish heads and innards by each bush. Her mother brought strawberry starts which soon took over a corner. Peas, beans, corn, lettuce, squash, onions, tomatoes, and pretty red rhubarb appeared in Mary Ann's neat little rows. The little gardener dedicated a large corner to her spud patch. There was a plethora of pansies bordering the porch and rows of daffodils to nod in the spring. With the coming of summer, the little house and garden had a happily lived in look.

She teetered slightly with her clutch of eggs. She was three, almost four months along before she shared her good news with Alden. She told him she felt fine and dandy, and that the angel of happiness had perched on her shoulder. Her husband was determined they would have a boy and made plans to name him Lyman, after his step-father and Ray for his little brother. Lyman Ray Ivie. Mary Ann agreed they were nice strong names of good men.

Alden worked for the forest service and there were times he needed to be away overnight breaking trail or fighting fire. If he was going to be gone more than a night or two, Mary Ann pestered her sister or mother or both to come and stay. It was easy to keep herself busy by day, but she simply did not like to be alone of an evening. With Alden away, the happy little trio would don their nightfrocks and sit fireside as they looked through Maria's magazines from the East. They pictured themselves in fancy, high necked lace gowns at lah-de-dah garden parties. Their imaginings would be brought up short when it was time to fetch another log for the fire or make a trip to the privy. They shared a morsel of sweet, a cookie or a dish of fruit, and sleepily put themselves to bed.

Of a morning, Mary Ann looked to the east to see the trees filigreed against the sky. In an hour, the fields would be a-hum with insects and Mary Ann would tend to her tasks of the day. She sometimes forced herself to a slow down a bit that she might caress her belly and think on the child growing there. The ghost of her little lost brother startled her as she reminded herself she would be totally responsible for the little being inside her body. She offered up a prayer. Maybe it wouldn't be too hard, God helping, to raise up a child with her husband beside her. It would be good to gift Dear Alden with a son.

Soup for supper. Bread and butter. A little sweet for dessert. I made do with whatever I had in my cellar or God gave me in my garden.

Mary Ann's Onion Soup

1/3 cup	butter
3 or 4	large onions, sliced or diced
2 tablespoons	sugar
1 tablespoon	molasses or brown sugar
1 teaspoon	vinegar
1 quart	beef stock or broth
	salt
	pepper

Cook onions in butter until they begin to brown. Add sugar, molasses, vinegar, and beef stock. Cover and simmer one hour. Add salt and pepper to taste.

Serves 4 to 6.

Seems dinner and supper wasn't finished without a bit of sweet. 'Times I opened a jar of fruit and set out some cookies. 'Times I made puddin'.

Mary Ann's Sweet Puddin'

2 cups	milk
2 tablespoons	cornstarch
¼ cup	sugar
2 tablespoons	molasses
pinch	salt
1 teaspoon	vanilla

Heat one cup of milk. To second cup of milk, add cornstarch, sugar, molasses, salt, and vanilla. Slowly add the mixture to the warm milk. Simmer 7-8 minutes. Cool and serve.

Serves 4.

If I had eggs a plenty, I poured off a cup of the warm pudding, stirred in one or two beaten eggs, and added it back to the warm puddin' in the pan. If I had cream a plenty, I stirred a cup of whipped cream into the cooled pudding.

Serves 5 or 6 if you add the eggs or cream. Add a little fruit and serve a crowd.

'Times I served up the puddin' alongside some fruit. Dear Alden was a trifle surprised when he figured out he was eatin' carrots along with his fruit.

Mary Ann's Fruit

3 cups	dried fruit, apples, peaches, pears, plums, cherries or any combination
½ cup	sugar
½ teaspoon	salt
2 or 3	carrots, grated
2 or 3	apples, grated
1 teaspoon	vinegar
1 tablespoon	butter

Cover and soak dried fruit with warm water for one hour. Drain and reserve the liquid.

Combine fruit, sugar, salt, carrots, apples, and vinegar with ½ cup of the reserved water. Bring to boil and simmer 1-2 hours adding back reserved liquid as needed. Finish with butter.

About 8 servings.

Pat-a-cake, pat-a-cake baker's man
Bake me a cake as fast as you can.
Pat it and prick it and mark it with B,
And put it in the oven for Baby and me.

Eight

Sweet Baby Mary Irma

In August I was with child, five near to six months. Alden and I agreed to share a wedding picture with my sister and his brother since we had missed the traveling photographer the year before. True to her idee, Mama had to let out the waist of my wedding gown. It wasn't buttoned up the back either, just pinned and sewed. My first sweet baby was on the way.

Mary Ann's mother, Maria, and a church woman helped at the birth. When Alden was invited to take a *look see* at his daughter, he asked, "Are you sure he's a girl?" They were sure, and they called her Irma.

Mother Maria put the baby to suckle at her daughter's breast. At first Mary Ann found nursing difficult, and she was fearful she would break the baby. With time she learned to be more comfortable in her motherhood. She was anxious to get back to her garden so Alden fashioned a cradle board. Mary Ann could papoose her baby and work about her home and yard.

Of a sudden it seemed it was time to make a one candle cake for Little Irma. Mary Ann was forever haunted by images of her little brother's death at eighteen months, so she did not breathe easy until she made Irma's two candle cake.

When Mary Ann went to the outside pump to wash her hands and face, the little one would mimic her and then dry her hands and face on her mother's skirts. She shadowed Mary Ann in the kitchen, learning to scrub and peel the spuds and shell the peas. Little Irma laughed as she repeated her grandmother's saying about the corn being extra good if you found a worm in it. She knew how to slap the ivory butter into a bowl and salt it some. She could set the table for three but became a trifle confused with the numbers when company showed up for dinner.

When she was about four, she crossed the front porch barefoot. It was early spring and she had not yet built her summer callouses. Irma collected so many splinters her poor feet looked like twin porcupines. It fell to Alden to remove those splinters, one by one, and douse her little feet with turpentine. She took care not to walk shoeless on the porch thereafter.

By the time she was nine Irma was doing the lion's share of cooking for the family and hired hands and relieved her mother to work in the field or garden. She was proud to turn out pies and cakes that rivaled Mary Ann's. Of course the little girl had a few disasters. She managed to get those messes out of the house into the hog trough, or out to the barn cats, or even bury them in the side yard before anyone suspected.

She attended primary school but never finished high school. She found her work and her joy on the farm, as she helped, did for, put by, and cooked for the family. Early on Irma decided when she grew up she would be exactly like her mother. She would marry a cowboy and have lots of babies.

Mary Ann's Pork Chops and Apples

4	pork chops
2 tablespoons	butter or bacon fat
1	large onion, sliced
2 tablespoons	brown sugar
½ teaspoon	cinnamon
¼ teaspoon	dry mustard
¼ teaspoon	salt
¼ teaspoon	pepper
2	apples, sliced

Preheat oven to 350°.

In a fry pan, brown pork chops about 4 minutes on each side. Set aside.

Cook onion in butter until translucent.

Combine brown sugar, cinnamon, dry mustard, salt, and pepper.

In a Dutch oven or casserole, layer onions and sliced apples. Sprinkle with half of the brown sugar mixture. Put pork chops on top and sprinkle with the last of the brown sugar mixture. Cover.

Bake at 350° one hour.

Serves 4.

Mary Ann's Cocoa Cake

2 cups	flour
3/4 cups	cocoa powder
1 ¼ teaspoons	baking soda
½ teaspoon	salt
3/4 cups	butter, softened
1 3/4 cups	sugar
2	eggs
¼ cup	molasses
1 teaspoon	vanilla
1 ¼ cups	water

Preheat oven to 350°.
Oil and flour two eight inch round pans or an 9x13 inch
rectangular pan.

Stir the dry ingredients, flour through salt, together. Cream
butter and sugar. Add eggs, molasses, and vanilla. Add flour
mixture alternately with water until combined.

Pour into prepared pan. Drop pan about three inches onto the
counter to bring air bubbles to the top.

Bake at 350°
        30-35 minutes for eight inch rounds
        35-45 minutes for rectangular, or until it springs back
        when touched.

Cool in pan one hour before inverting onto plate.
Cut into slices or squares. Serves 10 or 12.
Drizzle with cocoa sauce.

Cocoa *Sass* (Sauce)

¾ cup	water
½ cup	sugar
2 tablespoons	molasses
¾ cup	cocoa
¼ teaspoon	salt
1 teaspoon	vanilla

Boil water and sugar in a small pot. Stir in molasses, cocoa, and salt. Bring to boil and cook one minute, stirring constantly.

Mixture will thicken slightly. Remove from heat and add vanilla.

Cool.

Bye baby bunting
Daddy's gone a-hunting
Gone to get a rabbit skin
To wrap his baby bunting in.

Nine

Sweet Baby Mae Imogene

I tarried a trifle longer in the garden than I ought. I had no idee the second baby would come that much quicker than the first. My Sweet Mama was there to help, just as she'd helped with Irma two years before. For certain sure Alden had the right to blame me for dropping another girl, but oh how I wished he hadn't. Baby Mae wasn't a lick of trouble, and I decided right off she would be an outside girl, help her Daddy and all.

The little mother took care to step lightly over the creaky floor boards that ran the length of the room once she got her babies to sleep. The *girlies* looked like two peas in a pod and so reminded everyone of the Ainsworth sisters. Irma was dark like Mary Ann and her English father while Mae was blond and slender like Maudie and their Swedish mother. In her most secret heart, Mary Ann would have been happy to quit right there with the two girls. It was Alden who pestered for another child, a son. Sweet Mae was reared as an outside girl. Rather than deal with the inside chores, Mae was coaxed to follow in her father's steps, feed the chickens, milk the cows, and slop the pigs. She would learn to muck out the barn, ride a horse, and chase after runaway sheep and calves. It seemed somebody ought to help Dear Alden.

Sweet Mae was an easy child. Mary Ann belted her onto a chair and fed her oatmeal, shaving the cereal overflow off her chin. The little girl ate until she was full as a tick, then took to sucking her fingers for dessert. Mary Ann papoosed her on the cradle board as she had Irma. As she grew too big to carry, Little Mae was tethered to an outside post. Mary Ann was forever bustling about the laundry. While she sorted, sudsed, wash boarded, rinsed, wrung, and hung the clothes, she sometimes lost track of her babies. They were content enough to play in the posies and eat dirt. The little girls must each have eaten their pecks of dirt before they were three.

Up at rooster crow, it was time to halve the sheets. Mary Ann split the sheets and turned them so the less used outer edges became the middles. A little trick she learned from her mother, Mary Ann could make her sheets last twice as long. She ran up the new center seam on her mother's sewing machine. Glory be, that saved the time. Bed linens beyond repair were torn into diapers, sop rags, hair curlers, and *snot rags*.

It seemed that dinner interrupted her day. Of a sudden, it was time to leave the weeding in the garden and scurry up the big meal. Mary Ann had, of course, made her plan and started some pots to bubbling while she cleaned up from breakfast, but the final preparations often found her a little behind and always a little rattled and breathless. She made her music on the triangle to summon the family and occasional hired hand to wash and to table. As she whanged away on the twisted metal, she wished she could be making music on a piano instead. She reminded herself not to wish her life away.

Irma and Mae learned early on there were few pets for farm children. If they took a fancy to a baby chicken, duck, pig, or lamb it would likely end up on the Sunday dinner table. Their only almost pets were the barn cats and kittens that annoyed the birds and kept the mice at bay. Some of the kittens were tame enough to hold and pet, and Mama didn't seem to mind if the girls took some kitchen scraps and a bit of milk to their furry little friends.

Mary Ann hated the chamber pot. Her little girls were not allowed to use the thunder mug after age four unless they were ill. Mother figured they were old enough to do the necessary march and she was, after all, sick and tired of emptying and cleaning the piddle pot. The children hated the privy especially in summer when they breathed through their mouths in an effort to keep the odors from their nostrils. If they thought no one was looking they would squat and piddle behind the house. Mother tried her best not to be too hard on the children. Truth be told, Mary Ann loved being out at a picnic or camping where she could squat behind a fragrant bush to do her business. It was a little vacation from the evil odors of a summertime outhouse

Now the privy in winter was another story. It didn't smell so bad, but it was a chilly journey from the house and back. Mary Ann would sometimes find little patches of yellow snow behind the house. She forgave the piddling, but she would not forgive a mess. If she found one and could trace the culprit, that child was due for a whip of the willow to set the legs a tingling.

Spring and fall, with mild weather and no summer stench found the privy a quiet place to be. If someone needed some alone time, there it was. As the family grew Alden saw his daughters try patiently to wait their turns as they held themselves and did the *piddle dance* by the outhouse. He turned the privy into a two seater. So much for privacy. There was always reading material, an old wish book used for wiping. The boring advertisements for hardware and farm implements were the first to be used, but there remained pictures of dolls and clothes and jewelery and shoes to oogle and sigh over.

Tending to her garden, Mary Ann had dirt under her fingernails and grew large callouses. One evening she sat idly picking at her hands. She was disgusted with herself not only for the picking but for the sitting as if she had nothing to do, so she pulled out her knitting. She was just starting the toe for a new pair of socks for Alden when she was visited with a wonderful idea. As Alden wore out his socks, the toes were the first to go.

Much as she hated darning, she concluded she could simply pull the yarn and knit a new toe on the old sock. She was so delighted with her *idee*, she chuckled aloud leaving her family to wonder what was so funny.

It was almost Mae's birthday. Mary Ann's mother was, as usual, sewing up a storm for her granddaughter. Buttons, braid, and bows were the stuff of a little girl's dream. Relieved to be past two candle cakes, Mary Ann was concocting a five candle cake for Little Mae. As she stirred the dough with her wooden spoon, she said to her daughter, "Last day you'll ever be four, so enjoy it!"

I like to have sneaked vegetables in my suppers whensoever I could. Seems like if I made it tasty enough, my Dear Alden and girls would eat most anything I set on our table.

Mary Ann's Spud Pie

2 tablespoons	oil or bacon fat
4	stalks celery, diced
4	carrots, diced
1	onion, diced
2 cups	water or broth
¼ cup	flour
1 teaspoon	salt
½ teaspoon	pepper
4 cups	cooked lamb pieces or pork or beef
1 cup	peas
4 cups	hot mashed potatoes made with a little milk, salt, and pepper
2 tablespoons	butter
½ teaspoon	dry sage

Preheat oven to 400°.

In a fry pan that is oven safe, cook celery, carrots, and onion in oil until they show a touch of golden brown. Make a slurry of the water or broth and flour. Add seasonings and pour the slurry over the vegetables. Simmer until tender, about 3 to 5 minutes. Add lamb pieces and peas and heat through. Cover with mashed potatoes, dot with butter, and sprinkle with pepper.

Bake at 400°, 10 – 12 minutes, until potatoes are golden.
Rub sage between the palms of your hands and dust over the potatoes.
Serves 6.

In Mary Ann's make do manner, if nuts were scarce or unavailable In she used oatmeal or dried bread or biscuit crumbs to give that added crunch. She placed her dessert in the oven just before she sat to table so she could serve it still warm once the supper dishes were cleared. She usually served this with top milk or cream.

Mary Ann's Mixed Berry Crumble

½ cup	broken nuts, walnuts, almonds, filberts, what have you
½ cup	sugar, granulated or brown
2 tablespoons	flour
½ teaspoon	cinnamon
½ teaspoon	nutmeg
pinch	salt
1	large egg
1 tablespoon	butter
3 cups	mixed berries (raspberries, strawberries, boysenberries, blueberries, blackberries)
1-2 cups	cream, whipped cream, or ice cream

Preheat oven to 400°. Grease a 9" pie or cake pan with a bit of butter.

Spread nuts in a pan and bake until golden and fragrant. Cool.

Mix sugar, flour, salt, cinnamon, nutmeg, and salt. Cut in egg and butter. Toss in nuts.

Pick over berries and spread in the pan. Cover with nut, sugar, and egg mixture.

Bake 400°, 45 minutes. Let cool slightly. Serve with cream, whipped cream or ice cream.
Serves 6.

Mae's Peach Crumble

Mix the topping for the Mixed Berry Crumble, but spread it over 3 or 4 sliced peaches. Bake as directed. Serve with vanilla ice cream.

Serves 6.

Hush baby, my dolly, I pray you don't cry
And I'll give you some bread and some milk by the by.
Or perhaps you like custard or maybe a tart,
Then to either you're welcome with all of my heart.

Ten

Little Crookedy Girl

We named her Alsada Irene and she was born all crookedy like. Oh, she was a happy enough baby, suckled her milk, and 'most never cried. But when I first looked her over and counted her fingers and toes, I saw the bone run down her backside in a perfect S. When I showed Dear Alden, he said there was naught we could do but try to straighten her out. I took her tiny shoulders, he took her baby feet. Gentle as we could we tried to pull that S right out of her little back. We joggled her till she set to cryin' and we could tug at her no more. Each night we pulled her between us, just a trifle. We prayed we was makin' it better, and maybe we was. If she hadn't been pulled with love between us, maybe she'd have been a whole lot more crookedy.

With her first and second babies Mary Ann managed to take the time for cuddling and drinking in their little girl smells and smiles. When Sada came along things changed. For the first years of her life, Mary Ann referred to Sada lovingly as her Little Crookedy Girl. Almost forgetting her given name, the family adopted Mary Ann's pet name for her. Sada smiled a bashful little smile and fled to the barn where she played with the cats and their kittens. When company arrived, usually of a Sunday, Sada did her best to disappear. She was summoned to table, sat and passed the peas, helped to clear the dishes, then scuttled off again until the guests had departed. She seldom spoke.

When she was about four, Mary Ann took her little girl to town when she went to run some errands. The friendly owner of the Mercantile inquired, "And how's our Little Crookedy Girl today?" Sada smiled her closed lip smile as he handed her a stripped sugar stick. Mary Ann was horrified the shopkeeper had called her daughter Little Crookedy Girl.

"Her name is Sada," announced Mary Ann, and decided thereafter Sada would be called by her rightful name. The little mother remembered her manners and prompted her daughter to say thank you to the nice man. Sada looked at him, took a lick of her sweet, nodded, and cast her eyes in the direction of her feet. Mary Ann whispered a thank you, the words stuck in her throat. She finished with her selections, paid for them, and left.

Arriving at home, Sada fled to the barn as usual. That evening, after supper, Mary Ann told Alden what had happened in town. The family agreed to call the little one Sada from that time forward.

Now, meal times were quiet times. Alden had been reared in a household where dinner time was to eat, not to talk. All that might be heard at his table was the clack of wooden spoons on plates, the clatter of tin cups on the table, or the slurp of an especially tasty soup. Silence was occasionally interrupted by, "Please pass the peas."

One evening at supper, Alden glanced over to see his little Sada in a state of agitation. "Sada?" he asked. She looked down at her half finished meal and buttered biscuit and continued to fidget. "Sada?" he asked again.

"Kitties," whispered Sada to her lap.

"Kitties?" prompted her Daddy.

"Mmmm," she nodded her head yes.

"In the barn?"

"Mmmm," she nodded again.

Alden realized Sada wanted to tell him about the kittens, but she did not know how to proceed. She simply did not know her way around the language. Thinking on it, Alden concluded family meal times would no longer be quiet times. He would foster conversation among his children, Sada in particular. He began asking questions she could not answer with an "Mmmm" or a nod of the head. In time, she knew to look her father in the eye and answer with complete sentences. It was expected.

"And how was your day, my Sada?"

"I had a good day, Daddy."

"What did you do today?"

"I dressed my kitties in dolly clothes."

"I'm betting they did not like that much."

"They ran away. And hid from me," she added.

Alden encouraged a safe place for his daughters and their conversations, but Sada had difficulties most of her life talking with folks other than Daddy, Mama, and her sisters. She rarely went to school. As her days passed she shadowed her mother, especially around the stove. She was happiest when she could cook and bake and love up her kittens. She detested housekeeping. Although the exercise might have been good for her, Mary Ann tended to mollycoddle her Little Sada thinking the drudgery of homekeeping would most likely be hard on her poor little back.

Mary Ann's Pot Roast

1 tablespoon	butter or bacon fat
3-4 pound	roast
1 teaspoon	salt
½ teaspoon	pepper
½ teaspoon	rubbed sage
2 cups	onion, sliced or coarsley chopped
2 cups	beef broth and/or water
5	carrots, peeled and cut in one inch pieces
5	celery stalks, cut in one inch pieces
1	cabbage cut in 8 wedges
8	potatoes, peeled and cut in one inch pieces

Preheat oven to 350°.

Melt butter or bacon fat in a large Dutch oven. Add the roast, turning to brown it on all sides. Remove roast and salt, pepper, and sage it. Add onion to pan and cook until translucent. Return roast to Dutch oven with onion and add beef broth and/or water. Bring to a simmer.

Cover and place in oven.

Bake at 350° for one and one half hours.

Add carrots, celery, cabbage, and potatoes. Bake one more hour or until vegetables are tender.

Serves 8 to 10.

Sada's Creamed Peas

2 tablespoons	butter
2 tablespoons	flour
¼ teaspoon	nutmeg
½ teaspoon	salt
pinch	pepper
1 cup	milk
2 cups	fresh peas

In a sauce pan, melt butter over low heat. Stir in flour, nutmeg, salt, and a pinch of pepper.

Add milk and cook quickly, stirring as it thickens.

Add peas and cook just until warmed through. Remove from heat. Cover.

Creamed Peas and Potatoes

Follow the recipe for Creamed Peas but substitute 1 cup peeled, diced, cooked potatoes for 1 cup of the peas.

With her family constantly clamoring for sweets, Mary Ann often served this cake at dinner. Not often, but sometimes, there were even left overs for supper. If she made a layer cake, she usually filled it with jam or jelly and topped it with sweetened whipped cream. A rectangular cake was cut in squares and served with fruit and whipped cream.

Mary Ann's Easy Cake

Preheat oven to 350°.
Oil and flour two 8 inch round cake pans or one 9x13 inch rectangular pan.

2 ¼ cups	flour
1 ½ teaspoons	baking powder
½ teaspoon	soda
½ teaspoon	salt
¾ cup	butter
¾ cup	sugar
2 tablespoons	molasses or brown sugar
1 teaspoon	vanilla
2	eggs, separated
1 cup	buttermilk

Mix flour, baking powder, soda, and salt. In another bowl, cream butter and sugar. Add the molasses and vanilla. Stir beaten egg yolks and buttermilk into the creamed mixture. Stir the flour mixture, about a quarter at a time, into the creamed mixture. Whip the egg whites to soft peaks and fold in. Pour into prepared pan. Drop pan about three inches onto counter to bring air bubbles to the top.

Bake   at 350°
          about 20 minutes for two 8 inch rounds
          about 30 minutes for a 9x13 rectangular pan

Rock-a-bye baby, on the tree top.
When the wind blows the cradle will rock.
When the bough breaks the cradle will fall,
And down will come baby, cradle and all.

Eleven

Baby Girl Clara Maude

My first rememberin' upon wakin' up was the buzz of flies outside the windows we'd covered over with cheesecloth for the summer. Now who's to say what comes into a woman's mind after she's birthed her fourth daughter? Dear Alden was so disappointed. I felt puny, like someone'd kicked the pie clean out of me. I thought back on my own sweet Mama, how she 'most withered away after birthing little Albert. Then finally him dying, and her almost. Not long after, Daddy left us. I just couldn't shake it from my mind, me following right smack in my Mama's sad little footsteps. Maybe that's why I kept Baby Clara away from me, afeared I'd lose her. It was better not to love her if she was goin' to die. I was afeared I'd lose my husband, too. I stayed abed and tried to sort things out, but it was easier to turn my face to the wall and go back to sleep. I nursed the baby best I could, and wondered if they'd be hanging crepe for me, or if I'd ever be my old self again.

Almost nine year old Irma took her mother's chores upon herself while six year old Mae followed about, quiet as a mouse, trying to be helpful. Little Sada hid in the barn playing with her kittens, hoping Mama would get better and everything would be all right again. Mary Ann tried so not to waste the joy, but with each child she became a little more overwhelmed. Her mother Maria hobbled over daily to help where she could with meals and the washing up. Maudie came when she could, but she was busy with her own brood. Alden took to coming home earlier in the day. He did the heavy chores and brought in water and stove wood. He and Irma started dinner while Mae set table. Mary Ann stayed abed leaving Clara alone in the blanket lined box that served as a cradle when she was done with nursing.

One afternoon, Irma decided she and the girls would cheer Mama with flowers. Looking about, she discovered a bevy of blossoms adjacent to Mary Ann's garden. The threesome picked extravagant bouquets, came quietly into the house, and positioned a stem behind Baby Clara's ear. Mary Ann was napping, but when she finally heard them and rubbed the sleep from her eyes to focus, she growled, "Where'd you get them weeds?"

"Not weeds, Mama. Posies," grinned Irma hoping their offering would have the results she had planned. Her sisters formed a chorus of smiles and giggles.

"They're all 'round your garden," Mae finished.

"Tarnation!" she heard herself cuss as she hoisted herself on one elbow, then dizzily sank back in the bedclothes. Mary Ann could just imagine what was going on in her prized garden. She could picture those dandelions letting go their cargo of seeds to dance on the updraft and settle and thrive all over her carefully tilled rows. How could she let it go to ruin?

The girls and their offerings of those yellow posies eventually coaxed Mary Ann right out of that bed. She took herself for a brief visit to the town doctor in hopes of receiving a *fix it all tonic*. Looking her over, listening to her heart, taking note of her pasty complexion and the diminished sparkle in her eyes, the doctor shook his head and said, "No more babies, Mrs. Ivie." She found herself overwhelmed with feelings of guilt followed on the coattails of relief. How in the name of heaven could she tell Alden he would never get his boy?

On her way home, she ticked off the reasons to be done with having babies. She had four girls, that was enough. Girls were expensive. Although they tried, they were not so very much help to Alden on the farm. If she were to have another child, it would most likely be a girl. And no more messy loving, tired as she was all the time. No more worrying about awakening the sleeping daughters with noises in the night. Well, she concluded, Alden would just have to cope, as she would. After all, the doctor said so.

Mary Ann perked up a bit when she could get back to her gardening. She had missed almost four weeks of important growing time, so there was lots to catch up. She reckoned she could worry about the work that needed to be done or she could roll up her sleeves and get to it. She did not have time for both. As she returned to her routines, she kept Baby Clara at arm's length. Irma became Clara's little mother with Mae and Sada helping as they could. They washed her and changed her, dressed her in Sada's hand me downs, and fed her table food when she was ready. Clara was their own real life baby doll and was ever after their tag along. She was the apple of her father's eye, probably because Mary Ann *never paid her no never mind*.

Mary Ann's mother, Maria, wasted away and died the year after Clara was born. Maudie and Mary Ann tried to make her comfortable as possible during her last days. The bathing, feeding, medicating, and visiting was difficult for the daughters as both had families clamoring for attention. At the very end, they took turns staying over night with their Sweet Mama. Mary Ann was at her bedside when she passed.

She inherited her mother's sewing machine. Maria's other wordly goods, dishes, and linen were dutifully divided between her two girls. Baubles and keepsakes went to the grandchildren.

Now, Mary Ann kept a very orderly cellar. The glass jars were organized with older containers at easy reach in front and recently canned foods at the back of the shelves. The family sometimes ate from the stored jars in summer, even when fresh foods were available. That way, the jars could be recycled come canning time in August and September. Mary Ann had one she called the penny jar, hidden behind a tempting container of peaches. The glass held assorted coins and a few bills accumulated from selling milk, cream, butter, and eggs over the years. Of a Sunday morning, there was a penny from the jar, for each girl. The coin was twisted into the corner of a fresh hankie and taken to church as an offering. The little cache was Mary Ann's source of *walkin' around money.*

Unbeknownst to Mary Ann, almost everyone in the family knew about her hidden jar. Alden would occasionally examine it and add a few coins. The girls would look closely and notice it was down a bit come birthdays and Christmas. They knew better than to touch or mention it.

Mary Ann had been saving to buy fabric and lining for a new winter coat to replace the threadbare one she had been wearing for years. She might be able to use the buttons again, but she planned to tear the old garment into strips, braid and coil them, and extend the coat's usefulness as a rag rug.

One late morning while preparing for dinner Mary Ann went down to the cellar for some canned tomatoes. There she spied Clara, at about age eight, with the precious penny jar.

"And just what do you think you're doing, Little Missy?" Mary Ann was never one to mince words.

Clara was struck dumb. Not only had she been discovered, but she could hear pure wrath in her mother's voice. She began to stammer. Mary Ann cut her off.

"How dare you! Do you have an *idee* how long I've been saving? Do you have any *idee* what happens to thieves the likes of you? Run now, go cut a willow. I'll tan your legs something awful. You won't be walkin' for a week. You'll wish you never got out of bed this morning."

Reduced to tears, given no opportunity to explain herself, Clara flinched expecting a slap as she passed by her storming mother. The little girl found a sharp knife in the kitchen and went out to cut that willow. As she marched back from the marsh, she sat herself down to catch her breath and to think about what had just happened. She had never heard so much hate explode from her mother. It was as if her mother had stored anger for years and had finally let Clara hear and feel it all at once. Clara thought she could, she should explain to her mother just why she had been in her penny jar, but probably her mother would not believe her. She would call Clara a liar as well as a thief. The youngster decided to hold her tongue, take her whipping, and explain it all someday when her mother was calm. A little tingling of the legs could never hurt as much as her mother's words.

Clara walked back to the house and entered the kitchen where her mother stood, legs apart and hands on hips. Mother was still angry. "Well, Missy, what kept you?"

Clara took her whipping, wiped her tears on her pinafore, and never explained why she had been caught with her hand in the penny jar. Mary Ann knew she could not *unsay* the cruel words she had spoken in anger. She grew such a headache she took to her bed for a day, and Alden had to ride to town to fetch her a powder.

Dear Alden waited for his morsel of sweet after every dinner and supper.

Mary Ann's *Applesass* Cookies

Heat oven to 375°.

1 cup	shortening
2 cups	sugar
2	eggs
¼ cup	molasses
2 cups	applesauce
3 ½ cups	flour
1 cup	oatmeal
1 teaspoon	salt
1 teaspoon	soda
1 teaspoon	cinnamon
½ cup	walnuts, chopped
1 cup	raisins

Cream shortening and sugar. Add eggs, slightly beaten, molasses, and applesauce. Stir in dry ingredients, flour through cinnamon. Fold in walnuts and raisins.

Drop by teaspoonsful about 1 ½ inches apart on lightly greased baking sheet.

Bake at 375°, 9-12 minutes.

Makes 8+ dozen.

Mary Ann's *Applesass* Cake

1 cup	sugar
½ cup	butter
1	egg, beaten
1 cup	applesauce
1 ½ cups	flour
1 teaspoon	baking powder
1 teaspoon	cinnamon
½ teaspoon	nutmeg
½ teaspoon	salt
½ teaspoon	soda

Preheat oven to 375°. Grease and flour an 8x8" pan or a 9" round cake pan.

Cream sugar and butter. Add beaten egg and applesauce. Combine flour, baking powder, cinnamon, nutmeg, salt, and soda. Add dry ingredients to the creamed mixture. Pour batter into pan. Drop pan about three inches onto counter to bring air bubbles to the top.

Bake at 375°, 25 to 30 minutes.

Serves 8 or 9.

Toffee *Sass* (Sauce)

3 tablespoons	flour
1 cup	brown sugar
½ cup	water
pinch	salt
1 tablespoon	butter

Combine flour, brown sugar, water, and salt in a saucepan. Bring to a boil, reduce heat, and boil one minute. Stir in butter. Cool. Serve warm or at room temperature over Applesauce Cake.

Applesass Cream

1 cup	applesauce
2 cups	whipped cream
	cinnamon

Fold the applesauce into the whipped cream. Dust with cinnamon. Serve with the cake.

I won't be my father's Jack
And I won't be my father's Jill
I will be the fiddler's wife
And have music when I will.

Twelve

Dear Daddy

'long about after Baby Girl Clara came along, I was feelin'
poorly. I had such a time birthin' Clara the doctor told me no
more babies. Not a year later, I lost my Sweet Mama. Seems
like she had just embroidered the last pillow from my wedding
gown scraps for Baby Clara, and she was gone. Was I in a
sorry state. There was a terrible bad patch in our marriage. I
was stingy with my kisses and kept to my own side of the bed.
My Dear Alden kept his distance, and I forgot how to laugh.
Then, it seemed out of no wheres, I got a picture post card
from my long lost Daddy. His sorrow about my Mama's
passing rang hollow, so I took my own sweet time in answerin'.
When finally I wrote him, there come a long letter and an open
train ticket to visit him in Californee. Was I one excited missus.
My Dear Alden and his step papa, Lyman, said everything
would be fine and dandy. A trip would do me good. Irma and
Mae could handle the cookin' and cleanin' and washin' up and
baby mindin'. With my valise, two changes of clothes, and a few
necessaries I was up and off on an adventure almos' as excitin'
as climbin' that mountain of my girlhood.

Just as Mary Ann was about to board the train, Alden kissed
her on her forehead and whispered in her ear. She could barely
hear him over the thrunk thrunk of the engine and the hiss of
steam. All she heard was, "...miss you."

"Come again?" she asked, wanting to hear what he said.

"The girls are goin' to miss you." Alden did not plan to miss her. That gave her something to think about as the train pulled out and jostled her as it headed south. With the rhythm of the wheels on the track, there grew a fear in her head and heart that she just might lose her husband.

Mary Ann brought her book along for company. She had some crocheting to keep her hands busy. Irma had packed her a lunch to last two days and a bottle of water because the dining car might be too expensive. The little woman spent much of her train ride looking out the window at the fast moving scenery, mulling over Alden's words and their marriage. His remark washed over her like the cold waters of Trail Creek all the way to Los Angeles.

Her long lost Daddy met her train at the depot in a borrowed horseless carriage. As he handed her up into the vehicle, she felt almost giddy. At age thirty two, she had never ridden in an automobile, nor had she expected she ever would. The streets of 1910 Los Angeles were crowded with horseless carriages as well as the horsey kind. Trolley tracks crisscrossed the busy streets. The city was buzzing and busier than a beehive. She was almost breathless trying to take it all in, the vehicles, the smells, the colors, the noises, and so many people.

In his haste to charm her, James took her to a fancy lunch on their way to his home. Exhausted after sitting up nights to sleep, wrinkled and grimy from her trip, a fancy lunch was the last thing on Mary Ann's to do list. The travel costume she had worn was fine for Idaho but overly warm in the sunny clime of California. She so longed to loosen her corset. She hoped for a bath and a little toes up before facing another adventure. Lunch it was. Washing her hands before sitting to table, she took a peek in the mirror and was horrified to see the dust of the road settled in the creases of her forehead. She managed a quick rinse of her face and resolved she must not furrow her brow so much.

Her father rose as she joined him at the table. She swallowed her weariness along with her lemon water. James asked after Alden and demanded details about the girls. She caught him up between bites of food and swipes of her cloth napkin. She was grateful she knew some about table manners, thanks be to her mother, but she couldn't help but wonder how many rules of table she had broken. Was she allowed to use a crust of bread as a *pusher* to capture the savory sauce on her plate?

Her daddy's stories and the amazing food helped her forget how uncomfortable she thought she was. After they had dined, he drove to his bungalow set on the edge of an ostrich farm. In his excitement, he wanted to show her about the ranch, but she pled exhaustion. Once in the house, James introduced her to the water closet with its sparkling porcelain commode. Glory be! Mary Ann thought she had died and gone to heaven when she realized she would not have to walk outdoors to the privy. Then he began to heat water for her bath and she noted the water came through a pump, right into the house. She could not believe the size of the bathtub. Her tin washtub at home was *prett' near a spit bath* by comparison. She took her time bathing and hair washing, donned the summer weight frock she had packed, and collapsed into a nap that lasted until breakfast the next morning.

She awoke to the aromas of freshly brewed coffee, bacon, and toast of store bought bread. It was a bachelor's breakfast, James told her. Mary Ann found some guilty pleasure as she poured a little coffee into her milk to warm it a little. She relished every bite of the orange marmalade he offered to spread on her toast. She would definitely take home a jar of the sweet citrus jam for Alden and the girls.

As he walked her about the ranch and showed her this and that, she noticed he still peppered his speech with odds and ends of nursery rhymes. She wondered if he always did that or if he was still trying to win her back after all those years. When James left Idaho, more than twenty years before, he headed for California to make his fortune. Ranching and farming were all he knew, so he cowboyed for years before he won part ownership of the ostrich ranch in a card game. The major holder was not interested in the day to day running of the spread. Since James had been *to the plow born,* he learned quickly about the care and breeding of ostriches. He became the working partner and ranch manager.

He explained there was good money to be made in ostrich ranching. With no harm to the birds, breeders plucked the plumes that were used in the United States and sent to Europe as trim for hats and clothing. Poor quality feathers wound up as dusters. Eggs were gathered and sold. Considered a delicacy, one egg yielded an omelet for eight. Shells were carved and sold as souvenirs along with silver plated spoons engraved with likenesses of ostriches on the handles. If a herd, James never called it a flock, became too large, some of the male birds were butchered. Ostrich skin brought a high price as leather. Ostrich meat was quite edible, its taste and texture somewhere between chicken and beef.

Souvenirs were swept up by the tourists who came seeking thrills astride a seven or eight foot ostrich. James showed Mary Ann the saddles, harnesses, and pull carts he had fashioned for the big birds. As he explained the running of the ranch, a group of tourists drove up the dusty avenue and James excused himself. He answered their questions and saddled an ostrich he had captured from the herd earlier that morning. The would be rider promised he had ridden horses or James would not have helped him on the back of the more than three hundred pound bird. For the more timid in the group, James harnessed and attached another ostrich to a pull cart which could reach speeds up to thirty miles per hour.

After the satisfied tourists had paid for their privileges and selected some souvenirs, James offered Mary Ann a cart ride. Still dazed by the sights and sounds and fragrances, Mary Ann turned him down. She would have to think on it.

Next morning, she offered to cook breakfast. He surprised her with a four pound ostrich egg. She made an amazing *aggkaka* or Swedish egg cake like her mother used to make with the equivalent of twenty-four eggs. Mary Ann worried about the waste, but James showed her the wooden box in the corner of the kitchen, an ice box. He had ice delivered to his door on a regular basis, so he could keep food cold. Mary Ann covered and put the left over egg away, and they had breakfast for several days.

James still had the borrowed automobile, so that afternoon they drove to the beach. His daughter was overwhelmed with so much to see and hear and smell. Having never seen such an expanse of water, Mary Ann was a trifle frightened by the crashing waves. The swells and ripples seemed gentle enough once they reached the shore. James enjoyed himself as he waded and kept an eye on his daughter. After a time, she removed her shoes and stockings and fastened her skirts up around her waist. She exposed her legs to her knees and stuck a tentative toe in the water. She was up to her ankles when a pesky wave wet her skirts to her waist. She wasn't sure if she should laugh or cry. She laughed. Mesmerized at the comings and goings of the water, she tasted it just to be sure it was salt. James was determined to take his daughter to the beach again before she headed for home. With a proper bathing costume she might truly enjoy time in the ocean.

One thing about James disgusted Mary Ann. He forever tucked *snusa* in his cheek. It was a nasty little habit he had picked up from Maria's Swedish father. The Mormons banned smoking, but a touch of chewing tobacco was somehow ignored. She concluded her father was no longer churched as he enjoyed coffee and an occasional two fingers of whiskey.

James took his daughter shopping for a bathing costume and purchased a fancy bottle of orange toilet water as a take home treat for her and his granddaughters. Mary Ann opened her pocketbook and used her penny jar money to pick up a few doodads. She found a fine silk tie for Alden in shades of blue and gray to match his eyes. Some fancy ribbons, combs, and lengths of lace would bring smiles from the girls. She bought a container of marmalade to share with all. For herself, she splurged on a tiny tin of lip rouge. Her mother would turn over in her grave.

Mary Ann decided she would ride an ostrich before she headed home. She pictured herself sitting astride on the saddle. Of course she would have to hoist and tuck her dress as she had yet to wear a divided skirt. *My stars*, she had ridden her share of horses, skirts and all. James would have none of it, and he recited a rhyme from her childhood.

> *Trot trot to London*
> *Trot trot to Linn*
> *Watch out little girl*
> *Or you might fall in.*

Chuckling, he drew up a cart and harnessed one of the larger ostriches from his herd. He settled her in, handed her the reins, and she was off yahooing and raising hot summer dust racing around the ranch like any other tourist. *Mary-go-round-and-round-and-round.* She had the ride of her life.

Mary Ann's father took her to the depot and hugged her goodbye with a promise to visit Carey. He remembered his daughter and granddaughters with birthday dollars over the years. Come Christmas, the Ivie girls looked forward to the arrival of his string tied package of dried fruits and a jar of orange marmalade. James never set foot in Idaho again.

The travelin' took a heap longer than the visitin', but I felt the better for goin'. Dear Daddy helped me to understand how he'd pined away for my Sweet Mama, and she right there beside him. He could stand it no more, so off he went. He sent Mama money all those years so's she could put food on the table and buy lengths of fabric for her seamstressing. Daddy had made certain sure she could afford the silk and makin's for Maudie's and my weddin' dresses. She had what she needed, everythin' but him.

I made up my mind on my way home to Ideeho that my man was never goin' to pine for me to the point of leavin'. When he dropped me at the station Dear Alden had said, "The girls are goin' to miss you." How I wish he'd said, "I'm goin' to miss you." Well then, there I was headin' for home with a feather duster and gifts in my valise, tales to tell, wearin' an ostrich plume in my bonnet and just a touch of lip rouge. Wasn't I dolled up, and wouldn't Dear Alden be surprised to see me? I had my rest, I was feelin' full of health, and I would no longer be stingy with my kisses. I was thinkin' to finally have us that Baby Boy.

Maria's *Aggkaka*, Swedish Egg Cake

½ cup	butter
2 tablespoons	sugar
4	eggs, beaten
2 cups	milk
2/3 cup	flour
¼ teaspoon	salt

Preheat oven to 425°.

Melt butter in a large ovenproof fry pan. Coat the pan with butter. In a bowl, combine sugar, eggs, milk, flour, salt, and remaining butter from the pan. Pour the mixture into the pan.

Bake at 425°, 30 to 40 minutes.

Serve with orange marmalade or syrup or fruit preserves.

Seems like where ever I hung my hat and coat, folks was clamorin' for me to rustle up some biscuits. Got so's I could put these together 'most with my eyes closed.

Mary Ann's Buttermilk Biscuits

2½ cups	flour
1 teaspoon	salt
½ teaspoon	baking soda
3 tablespoons	baking powder
1/3 cup	butter, melted and cooled
1 cup	buttermilk
	salt or sugar or cinnamon

Preheat oven to 450°. Grease a cookie sheet.

Combine the dry ingredients. Add butter and buttermilk and stir to form the dough. Knead six to eight times on a floured board. Roll out to ½ inch thickness. Dust with salt or sugar.
Bake on a greased cookie sheet.
Bake at 450°, 10-12 minutes.

Makes a dozen biscuits.

Mary Ann dusted the biscuits with salt if they were to be served with savories. They were dusted with sugar and sometimes cinnamon if they'd be served with jam or jelly or used as shortcake. While in *Californee*, she learned to love her orange marmalade.

Mary Ann seldom made fancy cookies, but she made an exception at Christmas when she made her *Californee* Cookies. The original Swedish recipe was traditional to her mother's heritage. Mary Ann filled her cookies with the marmalade Dear Daddy sent every December. It was her way to get her parents back together whether they liked it or not.

Californee Cookies

½ cup	shortening
¼ cup	brown sugar
1	egg, divided into yolk and white
½ teaspoon	vanilla
1 cup	flour
¼ teaspoon	salt
1 cup	walnuts, finely chopped
½ cup	orange marmalade

Cream the shortening and brown sugar. Add the egg yolk and vanilla. Mix the flour and salt and combine with the creamed mixture.

Chill the dough

Preheat the oven to 375°.

Pinch off the dough and roll into walnut-sized balls. Dip the balls first in slightly beaten egg white and then in the chopped walnuts. Place cookies on a greased cookie sheet and make an impression in each ball with your little finger.

Bake at 375°
        10-12 minutes.

Cool and just before serving, fill each impression with orange marmalade.

Mary, Mary quite contrary
How does your garden grow?
With silver bells and cockle shells
And pretty maids all in a row.

Thirteen

Into Exile

Dear Alden was a sight for sore eyes, and he had missed me. I wasn't home a day before he laid the news on me. We were moving. Now, Alden had worked for the forest service since I knowed him, but we just wasn't makin' ends meet what with the four girlies. Seems there was a mine opened up in Mackay where Alden could get work to pad his wallet and make our lives a trifle easier. His step daddy, Lyman, had made a little scouting trip up to Mackay and found us a sweet piece of property on Alder Creek, just before it disappeared into the Lost River. The land and house was reasonable they told me, and Alden had sold the Carey house. I packed my necessaries and my cache of home jarred food. I near took my garden apart for the flower bulbs, rhubarb and strawberry starts, and pansy seeds so's I could make the new place homey. We loaded up our wagons, and quicker than you could say Jack Be Nimble we was off to Mackay. With the wagons, the girlies, and the livestock, we moved slow. We stopped in the cottonwoods to camp the night, and Alden tried his best to make us think we was on holiday. We settled into our new home. The older girls pitched in with the cleanin' and puttin' away. Irma, Mae, and Sada went off to school while Clara was still hangin' on my skirts. So I followed my husband to his promised land. Home was where my Dear Alden was.

Mary Ann, for all her busyness with home keeping, cooking,

child rearing, and work in the garden found traces of time to wallow in her own pity pond. How she missed her sister and girlhood friends left behind in Carey. Although she had received a luke warm welcome from the ladies at the new church, she decided to find her comfort in the garden where she felt closest to God. She named her little plot River Patch and celebrated the pristine waters that flowed past their property.

Mary Ann squatted in her garden, her head shielded from the scorching sun by her floppy bonnet. Years later, she would wish she had covered her hands as carefully as she covered her nose and chin. Crabbing down the row, she thinned the frail onions. Her fingers grasped just the right ones and she stowed them in her apron pocket. She would use the chives to season the dinner gravy. The onions that remained in the rows would thrive. She would harvest, dry, and store them in the root cellar come fall.

She turned her attention to the pea patch. Now, some folks planted their neat rows with seed planters, but Mary Ann figured her seed planters were at the ends of her arms. Peas and beans required less thinning, but there was always the weeding to be done. My how those weeds could camouflage themselves in her garden, stealing water and nutrients from her tiny tenders. She sometimes found a large interloper hiding among her vegetables, and she was always amazed she had somehow missed the culprit.

She weeded her way through the potato patch. Just weeks before she had busted the clods with her hands, breaking clumps to receive cuts of seed potatoes in early spring. *My stars, won't I have spuds a plenty come digging time!*

Absolutely no one was allowed in Mary Ann's garden. Those green and growing things belonged to her and to God. She felt the Lord spoke to her there and she so relished the alone time the tending afforded her. She weeded, thinned, patted, and watered as she scuttled sideways down the rows. Her vegetables and flowers never cried or sassed or needed to be changed or stuck out their little tongues.

She stood and stretched her back, leaned against her hoe, and looked north in the direction of Mount Borah. Her eyes of a sudden brimmed with tears. She bit her cheek in an effort to quell the quick sadness that overcame her. Her youth and spirit were represented by that mountain, and she wished she could climb it. Instead she mucked about in her garden, worried about her husband, and cared for those whining little girls. With a heavy sigh, she glanced at the sun over her shoulder and knew she must get a hurry on the irrigating. Then it would be time to finish preparations for dinner. She would tend to her posies later.

Come afternoon she was off to nurse her pansies. They were her pretty maids all in a row and how she loved their fancy faces. She sometimes pinned a brave little pansy to her shoulder which finally succumbed to the heat of supper's cooking. She kept a rose water vial and her marmalade jar, long emptied, at the ready for her posies on her window sill or table. Mary Ann delighted in taking along tussie-mussies as little gifts whenever she went calling. Although the tiny nosegays had originally been carried in hopes of keeping offensive odors at bay, Mary Ann fashioned the tiny bundles, tied with twine or bits of ribbon, simply to show off her pretty posies.

So passed Mary Ann's garden time.When buds burst in spring tease, she practically begged them to stay in their warm beds a trifle longer. When she determined the time was just right, she nudged her spring garden to life. She forever tended it in summer and rejoiced in its bounty come harvest. Although often overwhelmed by the work of canning, she took great pride in counting the full containers. She called them her jars of summer sunshine. As winter approached, she blanketed the root vegetables with straw that the family might enjoy winter overs fresh through December. Finally she covered the remains and put her garden gently to bed.

Since the passing of Alden's mother, Mary, Lyman had shown a keen interest in helping the young family of his stepson.

A true grandpa to the girls, he helped Mary Ann and made himself useful around the farm. Grandpa Peters made himself a little nest in the woodshed and took his meals with the family. He was not one to pass up Mary Ann's fine cooking. When he considered the farm chores done for a time, he put them to rest and took himself off to hunt or fish or explore. If the house noise of the giggling girls became too much for him, he would sit on the porch, smoke his pipe, and enjoy the peace of the evening. Sucking at his pipe one night, he remarked to Alden there was a sway back shed just hankering to be put to use. Plans were soon afoot to convert the shed to a bunkhouse. The door was repaired, boards were chinked, four cots were built, and a small wood stove set in. Mary Ann took in four boarders, single men who worked the mine with her husband. For two dollars a week, the fellows were housed, fed, and their clothes laundered. The foursome came for breakfast at the big house. Irma and Mae packed lunch tins with sandwiches of leftover biscuits and ham or bacon and a flask of water. In season, they added a windfall apple or a handful of cherries. Weeknights the boarders were on their own, but they were invited to join the family table of a Sunday for dinner. Although it meant *extree* work, Mary Ann refused to be overwhelmed and delighted in padding her penny jar with folding money. Her garden was thriving, and she had the girls to help with the laundry and meals. My stars, why hadn't she thought of being a landlady before?

As Alden's days passed in the mine, his healthy tan faded to an almost ghostly palor. He worked as a mucker and shoveled ore into the mine cars. His hands, although gloved in labor, were grimy beyond the help of soap. He saturated and wore out his workaday boots in the dampness, and he grew enormous blisters which turned to horny callouses under the heavy woolen socks Mary Ann knit for him. His uniform was heavy patched coveralls and a miner's cap. The hat was fashioned with a socket up front in which a candle stub perched. It would help to keep the dark at bay. Each day he trudged to the mine with his pail of lunch and a bottle of water. He passed his days picturing his little women gardening, going to school, and frolicking in the sunshine. When he came topside of an evening, the sparkle gone from his eyes, he marched himself home with a grin and hearty chuckle for the sake of his girls. He performed the necessary outdoor chores, downed a supper of soup or stew or spuds with meat gravy and took himself to bed to be ready for the next day.

Of a Saturday night while bathing, Mary Ann would fill his tub while she ticked off a list of to dos for the next day. As he soaked away the grime, he was exhausted as he listened to her. Before bed he stopped by the big room to see his little missies, all in a row, their newly washed hair wound up in rags so they would have curly dos for church next morning. He likened the show of white headed moppets to a mid-summer blizzard up Mackay way. A clean and tuckered husband would finally fall into bed beside the wife he counted on for warmth and comfort. Sunday, the day of rest, was filled with church going, catching up with insistent farm chores, time with family, and a big dinner. It was not a day of rest for Alden.

It pained me to think of Dear Alden who so loved the sun and out of doors working deep in that old mine. Why there was times he'd leave at dawn-dark, work his day in mine-dark, and come home at dusk-dark. I worried, but worrying didn't do nobody a particle of good. After a time, we girls got used to seeing him only of an evening and Sundays. Seemed to me the best I could do was keep our home a hummin', settle the tussles between the little girls myself, keep my garden goin', and give my man love and comfort as I knew how when he was t' home. In time, we was startin' another baby, our little man child.

"Looks like your Mama's been out picking weeds in her garden. Then she up and serves dirty soup for supper." Well of course I had grit under my fingernails, but how was a body supposed to raise up sweet talkin' little girls when their tease of a Daddy talked thataway about my soup? Well, I'm guessin' it did look a trifle dirty. They ate it and loved it down to the very last bean.

Mary Ann's Dirty Soup

1 pound	navy or white beans
	water to cover beans
½ pound	sausage
1	large onion, chopped
2	stalks celery, chopped
2	carrots, chopped
2 cups	mashed potatoes
3 tablespoons	dried sage, rubbed between the palms of the hands
½ teaspoon	pepper
1 tablespoon	salt

In a large pot, cover beans and allow to soak overnight. Do not rinse or drain.

Brown sausage in a fry pan. Remove sausage leaving oil in which to cook onion, celery, and carrots until they begin to brown. Add sausage, vegetables, sage, and pepper to the pot of beans. Add water just to cover mixture. Cover and simmer one hour. Add salt .

Serves 8 to 10.

I sometimes added a jar of tomatoes, just to stretch the soup a bit. Mae called it Dirty Pink Soup.

Lyman Peter's Fried Biscuits

Get some left over biscuits from Mary Ann. Split them, butter them, and fry them in a little bacon grease. Serve 'em up with Mary Ann's strawberry preserves.

I had a little pony
His name was Dapple Grey
I leant him to a lady
To ride a mile away.
She whipped him, she slashed him
She rode him through the mire;
I would not lend my pony now
For all the lady's hire.

Fourteen

Baby Boy Elmo

If I wasn't darned surprised, birthin' another girl after we'd picked a name for a boy and sewed up boy baby clothes. I reckon planning for a man child was like reachin' for the moon. We named her Elmo Rae, and she yelled and kicked like a cowboy. Cowgirl. I decided right off I would not be teachin' her to mend and cook and clean. She would be mindin' the stock, milkin' the cow, chasin' the chickens, herdin' the sheep, and mowin' the hay. I promised my husband Elmo and Mae would be our outside girlies 'cause we certain sure could not send her back. Dear Alden, he warmed to Baby Elmo right away. He said it was God's will that we be raisin' a fine crop of girls. I'm thinkin' sometimes you need a bad spell to realize how good life really is.

Eleven years older, Little Mae happily took on the care and feeding of her new little sister. Elmo toddled happily in Mae's shadow until she was old enough to be out and about with her Daddy. It came to pass that Elmo was an *outside girl.* There was no chore too difficult or dirty for Little Elmo to tackle. She fed the animals, milked, and mucked out the barn and the henhouse. Forever busy with chores when she was not in school, she could be found riding along with her Daddy or a hired hand just to take a *look see* around the farm.

Sada had her kittens and Elmo had her horses. Her very first mount was a wooden rocking horse called Sliver, carved and gifted by her Grandpa Peters. One of her early words was "Giddyup," and her second ride was the faithful old Ivie nag, Two Bits. The little pigtailed girl was ever eager to pack herself a sandwich of biscuit and ham, fill a flask with water, and skedaddle off with the ginger horse for a little explore or a fishing session up the creek. As she grew up, Elmo moved on to other mounts and was soon known for her ability to manuever almost any horseflesh. The big animals nickered in greeting, ate windfall apples from her hand, and kept still for her to climb aboard. She shared a deep trust with her horsey friends.

Some years later, Irma's husband brought over a frisky little filly named Flicker for the streak of white running through her chestnut tail. Sada was in love, but she was much too timid to try a ride. She begged her little sister to break Flicker. Now, Elmo had been hankering for a rifle of her own so she offered to trade a pony break for a smoke pole. Sada agreed. In two shakes of a lamb's tail, Flicker was gentled. Sada robbed her sock safe for folding money in payment. Elmo brought down her first buck with her very own rifle that fall. She was one excited cowgirl.

In her teen years, Elmo hired herself out as a wrangler. It was her job to care for the *extree* horses on round ups for branding and cattle drives from summer to winter pastures. Eventually she knew most every mount in the Little Wood River valley. She used some of her earnings for walking around money, but the lion's share found its way into her mother's penny jar.

Elmo did a man's work out there with the ranch hands. On our spread, she managed horses and was deep into haying time and harvest. Dinnertimes she ate along with the hired hands, and believe you me her favorite dessert was Cottage Cheese Pie.

Mary Ann's Lard Pie Crust

1 ¼ cups	flour
½ teaspoon	salt
1/3 cup	lard
3-4 tablespoons	water

Mix the flour and salt.

Using a pastry blender or two knives, cut in lard until pieces are about the size of peas. Divide the mixture into about 3 parts within the bowl. Sprinkle one tablespoon water over about a third of the flour and lard mixture. Toss gently with a fork until moistened. Push to the side of the bowl. Sprinkle and incorporate the second tablespoon of water over another third of the flour and lard mixture. Repeat with the last third and one tablespoon water. You will need three or four tablespoons of water.

Form into a ball. Flatten the dough on a lightly floured surface. Using a rolling pin, roll from the center to edges making a 10 to 12 inch circle. Dust with flour, fold into quarters, and lift into pie pan. Or lightly roll the dough circle over the floured rolling pin, then lightly roll it over the pie tin.

Proceed with the filling.

Double this recipe for a two crust pie.

Elmo's Cottage Cheese Pie

1 cup	currants
1 cup	boiling water
2 tablespoons	cornstarch
2	eggs, beaten
2 cups	cottage cheese, small curd
1½ cups	sugar
½ teaspoon	salt
¼ cup	cream, half and half, or evaporated milk
1	lemon, juice and grated rind
1 teaspoon	cinnamon
1 cup	milk

Prepare pie crust for a single crust pie. Do not bake.

Set one cup of currents to soften in one cup of boiling water. Drain.

Beat cornstarch with eggs in a large mixing bowl. Add cottage cheese, sugar, salt, cream, lemon juice and rind, cinnamon, and milk. Fold in currants and pour into a 9 inch unbaked pie crust.

Bake at 425° for 10 minutes. Then lower oven temperature to 375° for 45-50 minutes. Filling will continue to set as it cools.

Serves 6 to 8.

Good night, sleep tight,
Don't let the bedbugs bite.
And if they do
Then take your shoe
And knock 'em 'til
They're black and blue!

Fifteen

Borrowed Trouble

Mary Ann found herself tossing and turning, unable to sleep. She crept out of bed and out to the front porch step, clad only in her bed gown. She knew Dear Alden was worrying about something. She thought he might be fretting about the church for he had been summoned twice within the week. She sat on the chilly porch boards, picked at her nails, and borrowed trouble before she even had an inkling of what the trouble might be.

Little pockets of Mormons continued the practice of plural marriages in Utah and Idaho. Against the law but sanctioned by some of the congregations, it seemed everyone knew of a family boasting extra *aunts* and *sisters* and more babies of an age than most. Alden was doing well enough, maybe the elders had decided he should take an *extree* wife. The posssibility simmered in Mary Ann's mind until she thought it might boil over. She knew of the pain plural marriage had caused in Alden's family. His own mother had been a wife replaced. How could he?

She tried to count stars, the Lord's winking lamps. She heard Alden's footsteps behind her. He dropped the bed quilt over her shoulders, sat beside her on the step, and took her trembling hand in his. Silent for a moment, he took a deep breath and began to tell her the *goin's on*. His family had always tithed, but the church was demanding a double tithe since Alden worked the mine and their small farm. He explained to the elders the land simply provided food for his family and their livestock. He considered himself a subsistence farmer. That Mary Ann brought in a few nickels and dimes selling eggs and butter and housing and feeding a few miners *made no never mind*. Alden refused to pay a double tithe. The family would be excommunicated.

Mary Ann felt as if she had been punched in the stomach and the breath knocked out of her. For just a fleeting moment she thought she might die. Her brain could not wrap itself around that word, excommunicated. Alden touched her cheek in time to catch an escaping tear. She would have to cry later. Neither could think of any more to say. They shared a sigh, checked the stars, and took themselves to bed.

Mary Ann pondered their conversation for weeks. She could not imagine being exiled from the church that had given comfort since childhood. She could not fathom being separated from the community. Within the congregation there was no formal shunning, but Mary Ann knew old friends would drift away once they had heard. Why even Maudie and Ray and their children might keep their distance, for they were staunch believers and would never leave the church. She might lose her little sister to talk with, to lean upon. Mary Ann felt Alden was wrong but she was obliged to stand behind his decision. The church and the garden had been her worlds, the places in her heart where she felt closest to God. Her garden would be her comfort.

Ivie Ranger Cookies

1 cup	lard (shortening may be substituted*)
1 cup	sugar
1 cup	brown sugar
2	eggs, beaten
1 teaspoon	vanilla
2 cups	flour
1 teaspoon	baking soda
½ teaspoon	baking powder
½ teaspoon	salt
3 cups	oatmeal, quick cooking style
1 cup	coconut, grated
1 cup	walnuts, chopped

Preheat oven to 350°. Grease cookie sheets.

Cream lard (shortening) and sugars. Gradually add eggs and vanilla. Combine flour, baking soda, baking powder and salt. Gradually add the flour mixture to the creamed mixture. Fold in the oatmeal, coconut, and walnuts.

Drop by rounded teaspoonsful on cookie sheets and press with a fork.

Bake at 375° 9 to 11 minutes.

Makes about 6 dozen.

(*but they taste better with lard!)

Clara's Corny Cakes

4	eggs, beaten
2 cups	creamed corn
1 cup	corn kernels
½ cup	flour
1 tablespoon	sugar
½ teaspoon	salt
¼ teaspoon	pepper
¼ teaspoon	dry rubbed sage
2 tablespoons	butter, melted and cooled

Heat and grease a griddle.

To beaten eggs, add corns, flour, sugar, salt, pepper, sage, and melted butter.

Drop by tablespoonsful onto a hot, greased skillet and cook until lightly browned on both sides.

Serve with jam or syrup or melted butter.

For a more savory pancake, fold in two finely sliced scallions.

A nice little supper.

There was a little girl who had a little curl
Right in the middle of her forehead.
When she was good she was very, very good
But when she was bad she was horrid.

Sixteen

Baby Girl Katherine Ida

Up until Baby Kate was borned, all my girlies had been brought by the stork. Kate was brung by Odie.

After the excommunication, Mary Ann knew she could not depend on the women of the community to help with the birth of her sixth child. With her mother passed, Mary Ann harbored hope that her sister Maudie might come over and help. The morning she knew the baby was on the way, Mary Ann was out and about in her garden. The girls were off to school except seven year old Clara who was home with a croupy cough. The little girl stayed in the house while Baby Elmo napped. Mary Ann tottered to the house. Clara could tell from her Mama's pinched face and the way she held her belly help was needed. She lit out for the boarders' shed as she knew Mr. Hollander had not walked to work at the mine that morning. He had stayed abed with with an angry sprained ankle.

As he held Little Clara's hand, Odie Hollander limped into the house. In her mind, Mary Ann called him Odd Eye because he had one. His left eye wandered to the side and up and back again.   A person who conversed with him never knew quite where the eye would land. He claimed to have birthed cows and horses and sheep in his former life and so felt an old hand at the process. At Mary Ann's insistence, he sterilized the knife and washed up while Clara stoked the fire and set extra pots of water to boil. No one was surprised when Odie brought forth another girl. The pink infant let out a whoop when smacked her behind.

Odie cleaned up the baby while Clara washed and dried her mother as best she could. The freshly swaddled bundle was snuggled to nurse. Odie mopped his brow, glad to be done, and returned to the bunkhouse to prop up his sorry foot.

Alden came home and managed to hide his disappointment. Again. Mary Ann's tribe was ecstatic, except for Elmo who was less than happy to have her spot in the family usurped by a wee sister. Katie was like a brand new toy and not much trouble until she learned to walk and talk. The baby of the family practiced first on Elmo, then her other sisters. Finally, her hands perched on her tiny hips, Katie tried the little speech on Mama. "You're not the boss of me." Mary Ann never minced words. When she raised her voice using her daughter's middle name, "Katherine Ida!" the little girl knew trouble was headed her way.

I learned seamstressing from my Mama. She would make smocks of odds and ends, scraps from her sewing for others. Those frocks prett' near covered a body and kept the dresses beneath company clean. They had but two pockets. When I took to sewin', I made my aprons with a patch of pockets running the whole front of the apron, three and sometimes four across the bottom. Stray found pins I stuck through the fabric above my bosoms, and then I sometimes wondered why folks was hesitant to give me a good big hug. The pockets were useful, you bet, collecting pieces of twine, a comb gone missing, a bit of a pencil, or a stray weed. The trick was rememberin' to empty those pockets before tossin' the apron in with clothes to be washed.

Now, my Katie was a strong willed child, the sort to sass and stick out her tongue. A naughty little girl with a nasty little tongue. For her I learned to carry a little surprise. In one of my apron pockets, I put a pinch of pepper. The minute the words or tongue was out of her mouth, quick as a blink, I dusted her with a bit of the black stuff. Truth be told, I don't know if it was the pepper or just the idee, but it usually held her for a bit.

It was Mary Ann's forays to and from the garden that most worried the recipient of the pepper treatment. She simply could not help bending down to pull an intrusive weed from her path. With no place to throw it, smack into one of her pockets it went. Was that really pepper in her pocket, or was it lint or specks of dirt from the weeds near the chicken scratch?

It was a cold and frosty night, the kind of night when Mary Ann heated rocks on the stove, wrapped them in blanket scraps, and put them in beds to keep toes warm. Now, Mary Ann had a little saying that popped out about bedtime. As the girls were changing to their nightclothes, she would say,

> *Don't be wearin' socks to bed*
> *'Lest you expect to wake up dead.*

Mary Ann could not remember where she had heard it, or why she said it. Perhaps it was one of her Dear Daddy's rhymes. That night, Katie decided to accidently on purpose wear her socks to bed. It was a test. Socks would be a comfort on such a cold night. Next morning, the little girl pinched herself to make sure she had not woken up dead. So much for that silly little rhyme.

It was time for Kate's Saturday night bath in the old washtub. Through the evening, as the children took turns bathing, the water became appreciably cooler despite the fact that from time to time mother removed a pan of cold water and added a pan of warm. Now Katie, about five years old, had reason to believe she was the last in the tub. She decided to warm it up. Mommy only let them use the thunder mug until they were four, so by piddling in the tub the little imp would save a trip to the much hated privy. Katie finished her bath and was drying, when along came Elmo, her older sister by two candle cakes. Mother dutifully took some cool water out and added some warm so Elmo could get on with her bath. A delighted Katie ran to tell her older sisters that Elmo was taking a piddle bath. Katie and Elmo were usually in a tussle over something, so the younger felt she had certainly one-upped her big sister that time. Katie did it. Elmo basted the legs of Katie's under drawers shut. Tit for tat.

Mary Ann's Sourdough Hot Cakes with Meat Gravy

1 cup	sourdough starter
2 cups	warm water
3 cups	flour
1 teaspoon	dry yeast

The night before you are planning to make hot cakes, put your starter, warm water, flour, and yeast in a mixing bowl. Mix and put one cup of the starter back in the crock. Leave the crock and the covered bowl at room temperature overnight.

2	eggs
1 teaspoon	salt
2 teaspoons	baking powder
3 tablespoons	sugar
3 tablespoons	oil

To the sourdough mixture in the bowl, add eggs, salt, baking powder, sugar, and oil. If mixture seems too runny, add a little more flour. Stir only enough to combine and try not to destroy sourdough bubbles. Ladle and fry on a hot griddle.

Makes 12 or so, depending on size of hot cakes.

Gravy

4 tablespoons	butter or oil from the pan juices of chicken, turkey, beef, lamb, or pork
½ cup	flour
5 cups	pan juices and/or chicken, turkey, beef, lamb, or pork broth
1 teaspoon	salt
½ teaspoon	pepper
1 teaspoon	rubbed sage
	left over chicken, turkey, beef, lamb, or pork

Melt the butter and sprinkle flour over it. Cook and stir about 3 minutes. Slowly add the broth and/or pan juices mixed with water or milk to equal 5 cups liquid. Bring to boil, then drop temperature and simmer slowly 5 to 10 minutes or until gravy has thickened. Season with salt, pepper, and sage. Add leftover meat to the gravy and heat through.

Serve over hot cakes or biscuits.

Katie's Smashed Spuds and Cabbage

6-8	potatoes, peeled and quartered
2-3	slices bacon, diced
2 tablespoons	butter
1	medium onion, chopped
1	head cabbage, chopped
½ cup	water
½ cup	milk or cream, warmed
½ teaspoon	salt
¼ teaspoon	nutmeg
¼ teaspoon	pepper

Place the potatoes in a large saucepot and cover with cold water. Bring to boil. Cover and cook until fork tender, about 10-12 minutes.

In a Dutch oven, cook bacon until crisp. Remove with slotted spoon. To bacon drippings, add butter and chopped onion. Cook onion until translucent. Add chopped cabbage and water. Stir, cover, and cook over medium heat 15 minutes.

Drain potatoes, return to pan, add milk or cream, and mash. Cover.

Mix the cabbage and onion mixture with the mashed potatoes. Add salt, nutmeg, and pepper. Sprinkle with cooked bacon.

Makes 8-10 servings.

Doodle, doodle, doo
The princess lost her shoe.
Her highness hopped,
The fiddler stopped
Not knowing what to do.

Seventeen

Sweet Baby Edna Roberta

There she come, my Sweet Baby Edna, bright as a penny, my last stair step. Folks said having that baby would bring naught but comfort to my old age. With her older sisters takin' care of her and each other, my only job was a nursin' her and workin' my garden. I knew my baby havin' days was over and I said to myself, "No more babies, Mrs. Ivie."

Mary Ann was forty years old when her last baby came along. As a toddler, Edna could draw a chuckle from her weary Daddy when she wrapped her arms around his legs and danced upon his shoes. The little girl thrived and Mary Ann was delighted to have big sister Irma bake Sweet Edna's four candle cake. The seventh daughter was indeed bright as a penny until she took a strange fever that year. The illness was never named although some *suspicioned* it might have been a strain of the Spanish Influenza which had been epidemic in the country. Mary Ann was so terrified of the disease she liberally doused herself and her family with formalin, a solution of formaldehyde and water. Used as an antiseptic, it was probably the odor that kept potential germ carriers at bay. The girls were less than popular among their school mates as they sported *snot rags* pinned to their shoulders and wore their family fragrance, eau de formalin.

Edna's doctor was baffled. The littlest one took to her bed with whimpers and glazed eyes. Had she not been force fed,

Edna would have died within the first weeks. Her skin blistered and her frantic mother bathed her with baking soda in cool water, wrapped her in a down comforter, and prayed.

Now, Mary Ann was very protective of her feather bed. Chicken, duck, and goose feathers were always saved. When she had collected what she considered enough to make the job worthwhile, she washed, dried, and added the feathers to her double ticked mattress. She shook it daily and aired it weekly, if weather permitted, and only she and Alden were allowed on that bed. She broke her rule only for Sweet Baby Edna. Sleep on that feather bed was the only thing the worried little mother could think of to soothe her child.

Mary Ann sat beside Edna, knitted, and spoke the nursery rhymes that had comforted her own childhood. The sisters took turns to read stories and place soothing compresses on the tiny feverish brow. No tincture of benzoin or croup kettle could cure what ailed that little girl. Sweet Edna survived the fever but she lost her sparkle. School was always difficult for her. If she sat still for any period of time she would drift off in deep sleep. Her older sisters gently teased and accused her of playing 'possum. Why, she could nod off in the middle of a sentence, hers or anyone's. When she awoke, she had no idea what she had missed.

It was not long after Edna came along that Mary Ann began to notice her mirror was no longer good to her. She was forever surprised to see a middle aged woman, instead of the girl of twenty she remembered. Gravity was not her friend. Her hair was graying, her seventeen inch waist a memory, and her teeth were a misery.

Folks said you could expect to lose one tooth for each and every baby you carried. Well, I had chipped a tooth as a girl. It turned color so's I forgot how to open my mouth to smile. I lost that one, and seven more. I figgered it was time. The dentist, now, he wanted to rig me a contraption with false teeth that would fill the gaps. It seemed to me I had more gaps than teeth so I told him to take 'em, all that was left, and fix me up with store bought teeth. It took a bit of my penny jar money, but they was certainly worth it. They chewed good and they smiled good and I wished I'd done it years before.

Alden's hours at the mine were cut. The glory days of mining in Mackay were over. The bosses said the veins of ore were running out. Mary Ann's boarders quit her and were off to search for better hours and wages. Alden spent more time around home and rarely carried his lunch pail. As he shared more dinners with his girls, he encouraged more conversation while their mother pitched surface manners. Mary Ann reminded them she had been to a *hoity toity restaurant in Californee* and she didn't want her girls humiliated if they made a wrong move at table. The family always began their mealtimes with grace. It was expected the girls try everything placed before them on the table. They played *please pass the peas.* They were allowed *no thank you helpings.* When a dish was passed the second time, they were allowed to say, "No thank you." Although she could monitor elbows on table, it was more difficult to rule out the use of bread for pushers and dippers and soppers. It was especially hard to nudge manners when her own Dear Alden forever used a bread pusher opposite his fork and slurped his soup. The tired mother shrugged her shoulders and concluded her girlies would probably learn for themselves, the hard way.

During the productive years of the mine, families had settled up creek from the Ivies. The same summer the hours were cut, Mary Ann noticed her water supply had dwindled drastically. Weary, she set and reset her irrigation ditches in an attempt to squeeze out the last bit of the precious water. Her brow creased with worry as she found herself trying to coax a garden with less and less.

The alder trees and quaking aspen along Alder Creek

celebrated the fall equinox in their tattered gowns of gold and crimson. An early flurry tempted the girls to make snow angels. They succeeded only in making grass angels and stained their outer garments dirty green. As winter deepened and snow stuck, Mary Ann occasionally made crackle candy. She combined juice left over from her canned fruit with sugar and boiled it into a syrup which she poured over a patch of clean snow, much to the delight of her girls.

Mary Ann examined her winter creek. During spring run off, the stones were all but hidden from her eye. Late summer she leap frogged the rocks to cross over. The snow frosted stones reminded her of fluffy white bread crumbs, dropped by Hansel and Gretel in hopes of finding their way home.

Bless my soul, you'd have thought I was somebody's hero when I poured a little batch of syrup on the snow.

Mary Ann's Crackle Candy

1 cup	fruit juice, left over in the jar, peach, plum, apricot, pear, what have you
2 cups	sugar
pinch	cinnamon

Combine in a sauce pan and bring to boil. Cook at a hard boil about 1 minute. Pour over fresh snow.

Edna's Rhubarb Crunch

1 cup	flour
5 tablespoons	powdered sugar
½ cup	butter
2	eggs
1 ¼ cups	sugar
¼ cup	flour
¾ teaspoon	baking powder
pinch	salt
2 cups	rhubarb, fresh, chopped

Preheat oven to 350°. Grease an 8x8" pan.

Mix 1 cup flour, powdered sugar, and butter and pat into the pan.

Bake at 350°, 15 to 20 minutes or until brown.

Beat eggs until fluffy and add sugar, ¼ cup flour, baking powder, and salt. Fold in rhubarb. Pour over crust.

Bake at 350°, 30 to 35 minutes.
Serves 8.

Hickety, pickety, my black hen
She lays eggs for gentlemen.
Gentlemen come every day
To see what my black hen doth lay.

Eighteen

Exiled, Again

There we was, me and Dear Alden, our seven daughters, and two wagons full of everything I could think to bring. Alden told me not to worry my pretty head about stuff and things. Grandpa Peters had gone ahead and scouted a job for Alden at the mine. He found us a little house with a stove. So I didn't worry none about that, just ever'thin' else. Now we'd been up East Fork, just north of Hailey, in our honeymoon days, on our way to climb the big mountain. I remembered a pretty little valley. I remembered it smelled sweet and clean up there. But no pretty little valley was going to make up for havin' to move and start all over again. At my age. Why I was nigh unto old, forty and one and not a tooth in my head. My Dear Alden was starting over too, and him at forty and six. 'Course I had an understandin' of why we had to leave my sweet little house and garden down Alder Creek, but I couldn't for the life of me hit up my excitement for another beginnin'. As we turned into the little valley we would call home, I could see Hyndman Peak ahead to the east. I 'most cried thinkin' on my honeymoon days, carefree and climbin' that mountain. Then I looked around the wagonload of the seven little girlies come to us since and I smiled instead. Home was where my family was.

The East Fork of the Little Wood River ran almost silently through the long winters. Come spring the fragrant waters chuckled along the bed through the mountains. Summers the river fairly sang with the hum of insects. The summer song was

127

punctuated with the percussive plop of fat brown trout leaving concentric circles in wayside ponds.

The family was shoehorned into the tiny cabin Lyman had found. Alden and his stepfather set to adding a leanto for sleeping. Over time, Alden and Mary Ann kept the original addition as their bedroom and they added a leanto for the girls along with a cookshack. When the cabin was finally finished it boasted a little room for clothes washing next to the kitchen. Rather like a rabbit warren, a visitor could get lost in the hodge podge structure.

There was indeed a stove, if you could call it that. Tiny, it was meant to heat the one room they first nested in. A bachelor stove they called it, with space atop for a coffee pot and one pot for beans or stew. It may have been fine for a single man, but Mary Ann had to cook for three adults and seven children. She made do with her Dutch ovens and open fire in the yard and reminded herself it was just like a picnic. *Seemed like the smoke followed me, wherever I squatted to cook. But the smoke kept the 'squitos away.* She wondered just how she would survive winter making family meals in the open.

Their first holidays up East Fork, the little ones worried that Santa Claus would never make it down the smoke stack to leave their Christmas goodies. Alden assured the girls the latch string would be left out so Santa could enter their home through the front door with their presents.

Alden took himself off to work in the mine, and he labored on his new spread each evening and one day a week. Grandpa Peters made himself useful and puttered around the farm, but many days found him up the draw behind *the big house* where he fashioned another small cabin for himself. Much as he loved Alden and Mary Ann and the girls, the constant chatter wore him out and he looked forward to quiet time in his own place. All he hankered for was his own little porch step where he could sit and smoke and watch the sunset. When finally he had a roof in place, he ordered up a proper cook stove for Mary Ann and moved the tiny bachelor stove into his own little house.

Up East Fork, Mary Ann had her first opportunity to plan her garden just as she imagined it should be. She snugged the plot down from the house by the road. Nestled in the narrow valley, she knew she must make the most of sun exposure during the limited growing season. It was a bit of a stroll from her house to her garden. The climb up after the back break of a day's work left her breathless.

She amended the soil with buckets of manure and meadow muffins, forgotten and abandoned cud of cows. She designed a crosshatch of irrigation ditches fed from the spring up behind the house. Although Alden hired hands to do the ditch diggging, Mary Ann worked shoulder to shoulder with them to assure they followed her design to the last detail.

Over the years, Mary Ann practiced crop rotation only when the occasional brave volunteer shoot persuaded her a change might be beneficial. Despite the short growing season, Mary Ann expected her corn to be *knee high by the Fourth of July.* Her garden thrived thanks to her masterful planning and nurturing. While many folks suffered shortages during the Depression years, her cellars and larder were well stocked and her family never wanted for food.

Clara and Elmo, and eventually Kate and Edna, were off to school up by the Triumph Mine where Alden worked. The Ivies had a ginger colored nag named Two Bits, although Alden said she probably was not worth more than a plug nickel. Her back was swayed and her gait awkward, but she was dependable. She ferried the girls to and from school like so much cordwood stacked across her back. Mary Ann slapped the horse's rump and the girls set off with their mother's words, "Mind your ps and qs," ringing in their ears. The girls safely delivered, Two Bits returned the two miles and patiently chewed grass as she waited. Mary Ann reckoned on Alden's left at home timepiece and gave Two Bits flank another slap half an hour before school let out. The faithful old mare fetched the girls home in the nick of time for afternoon chores.

Work was hard but steady at the mine. Alden managed some over time, so he began to secretly stash some of his folding money. His Mary Ann had always longed for a piano. She had no *idee* how to play the instrument, but she was *certain sure* her girls would learn to play once she had planted a piano in her parlor. Alden saved for about four years and ordered a big mahogany upright from the east. It had to be shipped around Cape Horn and then about seven hundred miles from Portland, Oregon, by train and wagon. He had hoped to have it for Christmas, but its arrival was not possible until spring. Alden so wanted to make his little woman happy, to replace the worries that lined her face with smiles. He knew Mary Ann would be delighted to know her piano was on its way, so he fashioned her a Christmas card and enclosed a picture of the piano from the wish book catalogue. Mary Ann treasured that card.

Twice a month or so, Mary Ann took a morning away from her garden for a trip to town. She caught a ride on the miners' bus. The driver delivered workers from town, and he made a return trip for supplies and mail. Mary Ann knew the schedule, so she planted herself on the roadside and waggled her fingers as a signal to please stop. Beside her perched baskets and bundles for delivery to the Golden Rule in town. Eggs, butter, cream, and fresh vegetables were hauled to Hailey in trade. Mary Ann returned to the ranch with flour, sugar, molasses, oats, dried beans, spices, fabric, and notions that usually cost a pretty penny. The driver always welcomed the company of the nice little woman who offered him a dozen fresh eggs or a mound of freshly churned butter, perfectly salted, for his trouble.

The hottest day in August found Mary Ann elbow deep in the bushel of peaches Sister Maudie brought up from Carey. As she dunked the fruits in boiling water to slip their skins and ease the peels, she wiped at the beads of perspiration that bloomed on her brow and imagined what it would be like to open a jar of summer sunshine in January.

Mary Ann was known to play hooky from her garden and canning on the occasional summer afternoon. She and the girls would mosey down to the creek across the road. Cottonwoods and quaking aspen provided shade where they had built plank bridges across the marshlands. That pesky beaver was at it again. He dammed the creek where it suited his fancy, and his handiwork provided pools in which they waded and fished of a lazy afternoon. If they stopped and listened, they could hear the slap slap of his tail echo through the marsh. The girls frisked in the water, made flower dollies, and whittled willow whistles while their mother eased into her favorite fishing spot.

Following first freeze and potato harvest, fall winds roared down the little canyon from the east. Ice crystals formed alround the ponds, and massive tumbleweed graveyards were created along pasture fences. Those cemetaries were made all the more eerie when they were later blanketed by winter's first snows.

End of the week, seems I often had a loaf or two of bread go stale on me. I could whip up a little supper or dessert in almos' no time. Nobody never left my table hungry.

Mary Ann's Sweet Bread Puddin'

2 cups	grated apples
4 cups	cubed day old bread
½ cup	cottage cheese
1/3 cup	raisins or dried currants
¼ teaspoon	cinnamon
2 cups	milk
2	eggs
¼ cup	sugar
2 tablespoons	molasses
¼ teaspoon	cinnamon
1 tablespoon	butter

Combine apples, bread, cottage cheese, raisins, and ¼ teaspoon cinnamon in one bowl.

Combine milk, eggs, sugar, and molasses in another bowl.
In a 3 quart casserole, layer 1/3 of the bread and apple combination, ½ of the milk mixture, another 1/3 of the bread and apple, ½ of the milk mixture, ending with the last 1/3 of the bread and apples.

Sprinkle with ¼ teaspoon cinnamon and dot with butter.

Cover and let sit one hour, or refrigerate overnight.

Bake at 350°   45 minutes covered.
                10 minutes uncovered.
Let stand   15 minutes at room temperature.
Serves 8.

Mary Ann's Savory Bread Puddin'

2 cups	cooked pork, beef, ham, lamb, poultry, or sausage
4 cups	cubed day old bread
½ cup	cottage cheese
¼ teaspoon	pepper
¼ teaspoon	salt
2 cups	milk
2	eggs
¼ teaspoon	pepper
¼ teaspoon	dry rubbed sage
1 tablespoon	butter

Combine meat, bread, cottage cheese, and ¼ teaspoon pepper in one bowl. Add salt to taste. Combine milk and egg in another bowl.

In a 3 quart casserole, layer 1/3 of the meat and bread combination, 1/2 of the milk mixture, another 1/3 of the meat and bread, the remains of the milk mixture, ending with the last 1/3 of the meat and bread. Sprinkle with ¼ teaspoon pepper and dry rubbed sage. Dot with butter.

Cover and let sit one hour, or refrigerate overnight.

Bake at 350°	45 minutes covered,
	10 minutes uncovered.
Let stand	15 minutes at room temperature.
Serves 6-8.	

I was once fixin' to make the sausage puddin' for supper and threw in currants on mistake. I was teased a plenty, I should say, but nex' time the girlies was a beggin' for the currants.

There was an old woman who lived in a shoe
She had so many children she didn't know what to do.
She gave them some broth without any bread
She whipped them all soundly and put them to bed.

Nineteen

Company's Comin'!

'Most once a week one of my girlies would spot someone up the road and cry out, "Company's coming!" Seems folks always showed in time to sit with us to table. I aimed to be the good hostess rememberin' what my Sweet Mama said, "There is always room for one more at our table and in our hearts." Now if our company didn't show next to mealtime, I'd scurry up a little lunch for them anyway.

Isolated on their farms and ranches, the womenfolk looked forward to a little chit chat and catch up with family and friends. Sundays were visiting and company's coming kinds of days. Sometimes the cry was a false alarm. There was a fair amount of traffic to and from the mine on the road running just below the Ivie house, so Mary Ann had to be firm with the girls. They were not to call out unless a vehicle turned into their drive. She did not want to make a cellar dash for an *extree* can of peaches or tomatoes for no good reason.

She seldom doffed her apron as she knew she would soon have kitchen duty. As her guests approached Mary Ann smoothed her apron and hair and reworked her dinner plan, relieved she had harvested a full trug of produce that morning. Her slatted basket had all but overflowed with beans, corn, onions, and summer squash.

When Mary Ann served chicken to her family each and every part was spoken for, right down to the last piece over the fence. She hurried out to kill an *extree* bird before their guests had even set the hand brake. Before they had stepped out of the car, she had pressed the girls into service tidying, rustling up chairs, and table setting. Now, when Mary Ann and her sister Maudie went for a visit, they always took along their own plates and utensils. It was the Swedish custom taught to them by their Sweet Mama, for it was the rare household that boasted extra tableware. Visitors seldom brought table service, but the girls knew better than to bother their mother with details. They set the table to share plates and utensils among themselves knowing they could always use bread as pushers and soppers. The very little ones could use their fingers as long as they remembered to keep their elbows off the table.

There were greetings and hugs. Mary Ann chortled, "Well just lookie who's here?" even if the company was expected. There were quick exchanges of gossip and a walk around the ranch or a visit to Mary Ann's garden. The youngsters ran off to explore and play, and Sada introduced her little guests to the new kittens in the barn. The oldsters sat a spell to visit. Mary Ann bustled about her kitchen with Irma to do her bidding. Quick! Pluck the second chicken. Quick! Proof the rolls. Quick! Peel the spuds. Quick! Pour the tomatoes into the chipped yellow bowl, toss in some day old bread cubes. Rub a little sage over the top. Quick! Run to the garden for some green onions. She thanked her lucky stars she had made two *extree* rhubarb pies on her baking day.

After a general washing up, everyone found a place at Mary Ann's table. In the center sat a marmalade jar with a bouquet of her precious pansies. She and Irma put out the steaming platters and brimming bowls, and Alden led grace. The food was passed, and no one left her table hungry. A dinner for nine had magically become enough for fifteen or twenty. The girls were expected to pass on seconds and were silently forgiven if they said, "No thank you," the first time a platter or bowl came by. At a company table, their mother never made her usual pronouncement, "You'll eat it and you'll like it."

The sisters were charged with clearing the table. Those who would be washing and drying reminded the clearers not to stack the plates or their backsides would have to be washed, too.

Mary Ann prepared a little lunch of sandwiches and cookies to send along with her visitors in case they left her table hungry or got the hungries on their way home. The little hostess stood on her porch steps and waggled her fingers as they disappeared down the dusty drive. She made a beeline for the kitchen to survey the damage done to her larder and to rescue any possible leftovers she might use to embellish supper that evening or breakfast next morning.

Although home keeping seriously interfered with her time in the garden, Mary Ann was considered a masterful cook. For her generation, cooking was not a pastime but a way of life. As a child she had learned to be a gatherer of berries, a clutch of eggs, a handful of herbs, or an apronful of apples. Mary Ann and her little sister presented those found treasures to the mother who dutifully transformed them into sustenance for the family. Mary Ann had scrubbed and peeled her fair share of spuds and carrots and apples. If she found a worm in an apple or while shelling a walnut, she declared as her mother taught her, "It must be good. The worm likes it!"

Early in their marriage, Alden taught his bride the joys and mysteries of sourdough. When he took himself off to the mines, the entire process fell to his wife. She knew to freshen and set out the sourdough the night before. Next morning she divided the fermented foam and scurried half of it into hot cakes or biscuits. The rest would take the shape of bread or rolls by afternoon. Then the entire process would begin again. She knew the setting out of the sourdough each evening was as important as remembering to say her prayers.

Mary Ann never cooked with a mushroom. She had heard far too many tales of women who poisoned their families as they added the tender morsels of toadstools to their stews. She *suspicioned* them even when she found them displayed with the produce at the Golden Rule in town. There would be no mushrooms for Mary Ann.

As the summer sun buttered the valley, she rejoiced and tucked fruits of the season between rich pastry layers. She combined the ingredients for dough with her fingers, smoothed it into circles with her faithful rolling pin, and sweetened the fruit as necessary. With the final pinch of the crust, the shower of sugar, and bake of the oven, Mary Ann made the best pies in all *Ideeho*.

Company's comin' Sundays came, popped, and vanished like Mary Ann's washaday bubbles.

I always did love to see company come, and I was just as glad to see them go so's we could get back to our little life.

A dab of flour on her cheek or chin was evidence enough that Mary Ann had been baking up a storm.

Mary Ann's Butter Pie Crust

2 cups	flour
¾ teaspoon	salt
½ cup	chilled butter (1 cube) cut in pieces
6-7 tablespoons	cold water

Mix the flour and salt. Using a pastry blender or two knives, cut in butter until pieces are about the size of peas.

Divide the mixture into about 6 parts within the bowl. Sprinkle about one tablespoonful of water over a sixth of the flour and butter mixture. Toss gently with a fork until moistened. Push to the side of the bowl.

Sprinkle and incorporate the second tablespoon of water over another sixth of the flour and butter mixture. Repeat with the last of the flour butter mixture and water, adding a tablespoon at a time. Form into two balls.

Flatten the dough on a lightly floured surface. Using a rolling pin, roll from the center to edges making a 10 to 12 inch circle. Fold into quarters and lift into pie pan. Or lightly roll the dough circle over the floured rolling pin then lightly roll over the pie tin. Proceed with the filling.

This makes enough for a two crust pie.

Mary Ann's Rhubarb Pie

1 ½ cups	sugar
3 tablespoons	flour
1 teaspoon	cinnamon
1 teaspoon	nutmeg
2 tablespoons	melted butter, cooled
2	eggs, beaten
3 cups	rhubarb, fresh, diced

In a mixing bowl, blend the sugar, flour, cinnamon, melted butter and eggs. Fold in the rhubarb. Pour into an unbaked pie shell and top with crust (poke crust with fork to allow pie to vent) or lattice crust pieces.

Bake at 450° 10 minutes. Then lower temperature to 350° and bake another 25 to 30 minutes.

Cool before serving.

Serves 6-8.

Irma's Company Tomatoes

1 jar	home canned tomatoes or equivalent (approximately 32 ounces)
3	thick slices day old bread, cubed
	salt and pepper to taste
1 teaspoon	sage or a pinch of cinnamon

If time allows, cubed bread may be buttered and toasted before adding.

Pour tomatoes into a serving bowl. Add cubed bread, salt, and pepper.

Rub dry sage or sprinkle cinnamon over bowl.

Serves 6 to 8.

On Saturday night shall be all my care
To powder my locks and curl my hair.
On Sunday morning, my love will come in
When he will marry me with a gold ring.

Twenty

All Growed Up, Irma and Clara

*As the girls growed up, I had little heart hurts every time
one moved on. Irma moved out of our house but not so very far
away. Clara was off to teach primary school in Shoshone. Edna
and Katie and Irma's girls, worked down in Utah for a spell.
When they married, they was off again. I took my joy in
recollectin' the good times. I did love our Saturday nights when
they was all bathed and sweet smellin', the wet of their hair
drippin' on their nightclothes. They sat around the big room a
combin' and a brushin' and a helping each other to roll grand ol'
rag curls so's they'd all look bright and shiny for Sunday.*

*Seems like there was always big doins' at our house
Saturday nights. Before they started to chasin' the boys and
going out to dances over to the Grange and up to Sun Valley, we
had our own shindigs right there in the big room. We'd be
singin', playin' the spoons, beatin' out rhythms on the table and
the piano. They'd be practicin' dancin' with their Daddy and
partnerin' up with each other. Those old wood floors took a
heap of stompin', I can tell you, with seven dancin' daughters.
The old timey favorite was the two step, but they could hold
their own with a waltz or polka. Trouble was, they was so used
to leadin' must have given their fellas quite a time of it. We
laughed, we danced, we made fudge and pulled taffy.Happy
times.*

Irma

Now, Irma always said she wanted to marry a cowboy, so she up and married the boy next door. The new Ivie ranch on East Fork butted up against the Knight spread. Along came Frank Knight, a long tall drink of water, with a bandana snugged around his neck and his legs bowed from riding all day. He chewed a hank of straw that dangled between his lips, and Irma was smitten.

They married and settled into a little house, just up the river east of the mine. They had two babies right off. Mary was named after Mary Ann and was said to be the *spittin' image* of her mother and grandmother. Then along came Sweet and Shy Jeannie. No doubt Frank wanted sons, same as Alden. Frank took another look at Mary Ann's gaggle of girls and quit right there.

Irma was quite the little mother. She found it seriously gave her pain to hear a baby, any baby, cry. She would put down her own infant to comfort another. She had cooked since she was nine years old and she had shadowed Mary Ann all those years, so she was well prepared to be the wife and partner of a stockman and farmer.

Frank rode his own ranch and hired out to ride and rope and brand for other ranchers in the valley. In later years, while Frank rode the range and chased the white faced cattle, Irma cooked for the hired hands at roundup. She made do and cooked on a tiny stove in a refurbished sheepwagon. The heat of the fire coupled with the heat of the day would leave her exhausted, but when she struck that worn triangle to summon the hungry diners, she proudly provided the tasty *vittles the cowhands hankered for.*

I hadn't heard from Grandpa Peters one morning. 'Most every day he took a cup of coffee with me before he set out for the fields and I made my little weed pickin' run around the garden. I walked the path that snaked behind our house to his cabin up the draw and spied a big ol' robin a pullin' at a worm for all he was worth. Robins was good luck. As I came 'round the house, I found Lyman a sittin' on his front step, a leanin' against the post, stone dead. His burned out pipe was in his hand. I'm thinkin' he was watchin' the sunset when he passed nice and peaceful like. We all grieved, most especially Dear Alden. Lyman Peters was so good to all of us. We put him to rest with a stone pillow for his dear old head.

Clara

Clara was the first of the Ivie girls to finish high school. At seventeen, she graduated and took a job as a primary school teacher in Shoshone, Idaho. She loved to teach and be on her own, but she missed the good times with her sisters at the ranch. She knew her Daddy had a soft spot in his heart for her. Family meant the world.

Clara had a few days break one spring. A fellow teacher offered the use of his automobile that she might drive home and surprise her family. The teacher friend was careful to show her the idiosyncracies of his auto, taught her to check for water in the radiator and air in the tires. She even learned to change to the spare tire if, heaven forbid, she had a flat on the way.

She headed up the road with a canvas water bag hung from the hood ornament in case the radiator boiled over on the grade. There was a piece of road washed out by spring rains and runoff between Shoshone and Hailey, wide enough for just one car to pass. Somehow Clara stalled the motor. There she was stopped, fearful she might slide, with a car just behind her. She set the hand brake and tried to start the engine, to no avail. She had flooded it. The fellow in the car behind her honked. Then he honked a second time. After his third honk, Clara got out of the driver's seat and walked to his car. Peering through the window, she motioned for the young fellow to lower it. She gave him her biggest smile and said, "Hey! I have an idea. You go get my car started. I'll sit here and honk."

They shared a laugh. He eventually started her automobile, and they were on their way up the road to Hailey.

Irma's Chicken and Dumplings

1	chicken, cut up
4 quarts	water
2	onions, diced
2 cups	celery, diced
2 cups	carrots, diced
2 cups	corn
2-3 cups	potatoes, diced
1 tablespoon	salt
½ teaspoon	pepper
1 teaspoon	sage, rubbed between palms over soup
1 recipe	dumplings

Place chicken in a large Dutch oven or soup pot and cover with water. Bring to boil and simmer until tender, about one hour. Remove chicken from heat and allow to cool. Remove meat from the bones and cut into bite sized pieces. Discard the skin and bones. Skim the fat as the broth cools and discard. Return broth to a simmer and add vegetables and chicken pieces. Simmer about 15 minutes. Add dumplings. Simmer 15 to 20 more minutes.

Swedish Dumplings

1 cup	milk
1 cup	flour
1	egg
½ teaspoon	salt

In a small saucepot, mix milk and flour and cook until thick. Cool slightly. Stir in egg and salt. Drop by teaspoonsful into broth.

When she was t' home, Irma pleased her family with fancy desserts. Dinner wasn't no dinner without a sweet finish at Irma's.

Irma's Cream Puffs

1/3 cup	butter
1 cup	water
1 cup	flour
4	eggs

Preheat oven to 400°. Grease a cookie sheet or 12 cup muffin pan.
Bring the butter and water to a boil. Add flour stirring constantly. It will form a stiff dough. Let stand a few minutes to cool. Stir in one egg at a time, beating constantly, until all four eggs are incorporated.

Pile on greased cookie sheet or into greased muffin pans.

Bake at 400° for 20 minutes. Lower temperature to 325° and bake 25 minutes more.

When cool, split and discard the doughy centers. Allow puffs to dry.

Fill with whipped cream, adjust tops, and dust with powdered sugar. These may be filled with pudding or berries.

Clara's Brownies

4	eggs
1 cup	sugar
1 cup	brown sugar
½ cup	butter, melted and cooled (1 cube)
1 cup	flour
¾ cup	cocoa
½ teaspoon	salt
1 teaspoon	vanilla
½ cup	walnuts, broken, optional

Preheat oven to 325°. Butter and flour an 8x8" pan.

Beat the eggs until fluffy. Add sugar, butter, flour, cocoa, salt, and vanilla. Nuts may be folded in.

Pour into pan. Drop pan about three inches onto counter to bring air bubbles to the top.

Bake at 325° for 25-35 minutes.

Cool before cutting.

Makes about 16 two-inch brownies.

The little robin grieves
When the snow is on the ground,
For the trees have no leaves
And no berries can be found.

Twenty-one

Crosses to Bear

In April of 1928, when Clara was just twenty years old, she caught a cold which turned to pneumonia. A colleague told the family she had lent her heavy outer coat to a student who had come to school without. In a matter of days she was gone.

At her funeral, Clara looked serene in her casket with a lily in her youthful hands. She might have been just asleep. Mary Ann tucked a bell in her resting box that Clara might ring if she were alive. A traditional bell had been placed in her Sweet Mother's casket almost twenty years before.

The letter addressed to Mary Ann was at the post office the day of the funeral. Alden and a weeping Mary Ann stopped for the mail on their way home from the cemetary. When she saw the post mark and return address the grieving mother knew it was from her Clara. For a flicker of a moment Mary Ann thought maybe they hadn't buried their little girl, that it was all just a nightmare, a mistake. She tucked the letter in her bosom, over her heart, to read later.

When the funeral visitors had gone she sat herself down to read.

30 March 1928
Mama dear,
I have always wanted to tell you how sorry I was about your penny jar. I wanted you to know what happened that day. I hoped you'd listen then, but you made up your mind before the

words were out of my mouth.

Mama, I was putting money into the jar, not taking it out. Do you remember, after you visited your Daddy in California, how he sent us girls money for our birthdays? You were saving for a new winter coat. You hadn't had a new one in a long time. So when I got my birthday dollar, I bought a book in town for me and some lemon drops to share with the girls. The extra coins I took to the cellar. I knew where your money jar was. We all knew. I was just screwing the lid back on when you caught me.

You didn't believe me then, but so many years have passed. You have seen that I turned out to be a good person. So maybe you'll believe me now.

I love you, and I am sorry for whatever I've done bad. I hope you and Daddy are well. I think about you all the time. I miss you and Daddy and the ranch and my sisters. It is probably a good thing, though, me being away.

Your loving daughter, Clara

Mary Ann felt as if she had been kicked in the breadbasket. Her face crumpled and as her eyes brimmed with tears, she passed the letter to Alden. She expected words of comfort so she was horrified by the anger in his voice. "My good God, Mary Ann, and you've punished her all these years?"

Mary Ann could never *unsay* the words she had spouted at her Little Clara in anger all those years ago. Nor could Alden take his back. His words hung like a heavy dark cloud curtain between the couple. Alden went back to the mine the day after the funeral. Mary Ann took herself to bed and hoped to sleep forever.

A few weeks passed. Alden, grieving over Clara's death and still upset with his wife, paid *no never mind* to the dangerous work he was about. A run away ore car caught him and crushed him from the heart down. He was alive when they took him to town in the back of a pickup truck. He was alive when his brother and cousins came up from Carey and insisted that he be moved there where he had been churched. Too distraught to intervene, Mary Ann held his hand tightly in both of hers and said over and over, "I'm so sorry. I'm so sorry." He passed in Carey, but the cousins brought him home to rest next to his daughter in Hailey. He was buried on his birthday in a closed casket to hide his final pain. He had no need for a bell.

Mary Ann wrapped herself in a blanket of grief and planted herself in the bed she had shared with her Alden for almost thirty years. She wept until she slept. Mornings when Mary Ann awakened, there was a fleeting instant when all seemed well with the world. Then it all came back on her. It was as if she were crushed by that runaway mine car. The overwhelming sadness washed over her again and again. How many mornings would she suffer such torment? The worst of it was she had never made amends with her daughter or husband. Only angry words had been spoken. Mary Ann pictured her Dear Alden, her Sweet Mama, Lyman, and Sweet Clara having a little chat with God about all her rights and wrongs. Please God, she prayed the goods outweighed the bads. She was so deep in her own heartache she had nothing left to offer the girls who cried for their sister and father. They were left to comfort each other.

Mary Ann chose the stone pillows for the graves. When the markers were placed, she scarcely noticed the little cemetary was lush with wildflowers.

She would have slept the rest of her life away if she had not faced up to the responsibility of the ranch and the girls still at home. With Irma married off to Frank, she had Mae, Sada, Elmo, Kate, and Edna to do for. How much easier it would have been to turn tail and run. Truth be told, somedays she did just that. She would finish her chores of a morning. She would wash up and eat the dinner Sada had put on the table with ten year old Edna's help. She checked in with her Outside Girls, Mae, Elmo, and Kate to see what was doing or needed to be done. Would they need one hired hand or two to bring in the hay? Had anyone ridden and checked the south fence line? Then she gathered her fishing gear and headed downhill in the direction of the creek. In the peace and quiet of late day, she wrapped her mind around the crosses she must bear. After a time, she learned she must remember the happy times and put away the sad. As a child, when she had chipped her tooth, she had learned to smile with her mouth closed. For years the grieving wife and mother smiled with her heart closed.

I got to thinkin' my sores would never scab over. I missed my Dear Alden, and it just wasn't right for a mother to outlive a child. Maudie and Ray had their family sealed at the Mormon temple so's they'd all find each other in heaven. I wished I'd had that comfort.

Some summer afternoons I learned to take time from my garden without feeling so very guilty. I laced up my boots, grabbed my fishing hat and creel, and headed down to the creek to drown a few worms. There I was all alone with my thoughts. I could cry for my Dear Alden and devil myself with should haves for my little Clara lost to pneumonee. I took a look see at some idees I'd put away to ponder. And with a little luck, we had us a mess o' trout for supper.

I always took the heads clean off my trout. I didn't like my food lookin' at me.

Mess o' Trout

4	trout, cleaned and headed (leave tail on)
½ cup	flour, divided
1	egg, beaten
1 teaspoon	salt
½ teaspoon	pepper
1 teaspoon	sage, dried and crushed
¼ cup	oil, lard, or bacon grease for frying

Leave ¼ cup of the flour plain. Add salt, pepper, and dried sage to the other ¼ cup. Lay out three plates: plain flour, beaten egg, seasoned flour.

Heat oil until drops of water dance and sizzle.

Dredge the trout, both sides, in plain flour, egg, then seasoned flour. Fry in pan until skin is golden brown and the fish flakes.

Place on serving plate. Open, grip the tail, and gently pull bones out of the fish.

Serves 4.

Mary Ann was pleased and proud to bring home *a mess o' trout*, and her Spud and Cheese Pie was the perfect side dish.

Mary Ann's Spud and Cheese Pie

6	potatoes, peeled and sliced thin
2 cups	cheese, grated
3 tablespoons	butter, melted
	salt, pepper, sage
¾ cup	milk

Preheat oven to 425°.

In a greased ovenproof casserole or large pie pan, layer the butter, potatoes, cheese, salt, pepper, and sage three times.

Pour milk over the top.

Bake at 425° for 45 minutes or until brown on top and liquid is absorbed.

Serves 6-8.

Girls and boys come out to play,
The moon doth shine as bright as day.
Leave your supper and leave your sleep
And come with your playfellows into the street.

Twenty-two

The Outside Girls

My sister Maudie and Ray had themselves a passel of children, too. Three boys and three girls. Me and Maudie worried a titch about my Elmo and her second son. When they was children, they had time and eyes only for each other, and when they got older they found all sorts of excuses to go off and be together. Cousin marriages were frowned on, but a double cousin weddin' would be a sure calamity.

Saturday nights the girls got all dolled up. Pretty is as pretty does, I reminded my girlies. Beauty is only skin deep. I'm thinkin' it all fell on deaf ears.

Silk was at a premium during the war as the fabric was used for parachutes. The sisters followed the fashion and captured the look of silk stockings by drawing lines down the backs of their legs before heading out to dates and dances. They helped each other to draw the seams straight and keep the lines from smudging. A giggling and chatting point was just how far up the legs those seam lines should be drawn.

Mae

Mae took herself to Oregon where she worked for a doctor and his family. Home for a visit one day, she chanced to be in town with Katie. Sitting and waiting for her sister in the car, she looked up to see a man walking in her direction. She chuckled to herself at how very stiff he looked for such a young man, as if a lodge pole pine had been stuck down his back.

He walked right up to the open passenger window clearly on a mission. Mae thought perhaps one of the tires needed air. She rolled down her window and he bent that stiff back over, introduced himself, and asked her to go to the dance in town Saturday night. She was so surprised, she could think of nothing to say, so she smiled. She began to introduce herself and the man of few words said, "I know. You're Mae Ivie. Up East Fork. Name's Henry Brasse. I'll call for you at seven." He'd had his eye on the second sister for quite a spell.

When Katie came back to the car and slid into the driver's seat, Mae laughed out loud and told her, "I do believe I just made a date with Old Stiff Neck. What ever made me do that?" she wondered.

Well, she up and married that Henry Brasse. They bought a little spread up East Fork, just west of the Ivie ranch on the creek side of the road. Henry divided his time between ranching and working at the mine, and he installed one of the first bathrooms in the little farm community. No privy for Sweet Mae.

Their first baby, Gerald, died just after he was born with the umbilical cord wrapped around his tiny neck. Two years later, Rodney came howling into the world. Mary Ann was one excited Grandma. *My stars!* After all those years she had hankered for a son and and ended up with seven girlies and two girl grandbabies. The man child was healthy, life was good, and she felt so very blessed.

Henry was milking the big guernsey in the barn one evening when he was joined by two little on-lookers, the city kids. He easily convinced the children that each of the four spigots on the cow's udder held a different beverage. White milk, chocolate milk, buttermilk, and *sodee pop* were available if you just knew which teat to squeeze. "Let me show you," and he proved it by shooting a spray of milk at them. Laughing, the children begged to sample the chocolate milk and soda pop. Henry apologized and explained those spigots were not working that particular day.

Elmo

At fifteen years, just a year after she lost her Daddy and big sister, Clara, Elmo was off to town for high school. It was too far to travel from the ranch into Hailey each day, so arrangements were made with some of the town folk for the farm kids to board weekdays in exchange for chores and babysitting. Elmo landed with the Blankenships, an old time Hailey family. In exchange for her space, she did child care, some cooking, and lots of cleaning. Having always been an outside girl, the domesticity was a bit of a stretch for the young girl. She arrived in town Sunday evenings and returned home of a Friday afternoon. With a "Wahoo!" she felt like a horse headed for the barn. She loved school, but she detested her living situation. It was good to be home.

She won awards for her typing speed and accuracy, so her next step was to work in the forest service office. She spent most of her free time at the ranch, where she broke horses, brought in the hay, or tackled whatever outside chores called to be done.

Elmo used hearts like stepping stones. She learned early on that if she was engaged she was guaranteed a date for Saturday night although she had no qualms about going to dances solo. She was not as selective as her mother and sisters thought she should be. They were *certain sure* one of her suitors was dumb as a post and another fellow talked just to hear his head rattle.

One Saturday night, while engaged, she went to the big dance in Sun Valley with Kate and some girlfriends. An older man with a funny Swedish accent and the kindest hazel eyes asked her to dance. When he neglected to call her that week, she joked with her sisters about his big floppy ears and huge honker that almost matched his maroon tie. He was up from Los Angeles and he worked on the construction crew at the Inn. They met up again at another dance. Within a few weeks she broke her engagement, she and Emil became an item, and they eloped that December.

I had some regrets sending Elmo off to Californee with an older man, him bein' a foreigner to boot, and her not knowing much about home keepin' and cookin'. She never did learn to manage sourdough. Her bein' an outside girl, she'd never taken to worryin' about such. We knew there was no stoppin' her once she'd made up her mind. Emil Erlandson was her steppin' stone clean out of Ideeho.

So Elmo became a city girl. She and her new husband made Los Angeles their home base, but his work took him north to the Monterey area where he worked on the bridge near Big Sur. They traveled east to Nevada where he crewed on the construction of a magnesium plant. Elmo went along, happy to be on the move as she learned to be a city slicker.

Now, she had known when they married that Emil was divorced with two children. He explained his children, a boy and a girl, lived with relatives. Although Emil thought the children were fine and dandy where they were, his relatives had other ideas. They concluded the newlyweds could and should take on the responsibility. So a twenty six year old Elmo suddenly had a teenage son and daughter, Ralph and Lila. Emil thought two was plenty, but Elmo was determined to have babies of her own. Five years after they were married, they had Little Rae. Two years later, they welcomed Dear Denny.

There were no regrets for Elmo when she left the harsh winters of Idaho, but she did miss the summers and her family. For all her city mouse ways, Elmo couldn't wait to *get up t' home* to catch up and gossip and picnic with her sisters and mother. As she drove east, her children counted the Ts of the telephone poles that marched across the landscape. Elmo took in the passing fields fenced in fits and starts that hemmed the highway. In her haste, her foot sometimes got a trifle heavy on the accelerator. Under her breath she murmured, "Whoa little horsey," and eased up on the gas. When she turned north at Shoshone and set eyes on the familiar layered crags of the

Sawtooth Mountains she shouted a "Wahoo!" that spiraled all the way up from her toes.Peek-a-boo views of those mountains teased her all the way to Hailey. Wahoo! She was home.

Kate

Katie followed her big sister Elmo to Hailey, lived in town to go to high school, graduated, and busied herself with all manner of jobs. She clerked at the grocery and waitressed along with her little sister, Edna. She followed in Elmo's footsteps again when she snagged a job with the forest service. The young woman filed, typed, answered phone, and operated the two way radio. Some boss had himself a Girl Friday.

The radio connected her office with the rangers. Out and about the men monitored campgrounds, broke and maintained trails, and watched for fires from the towers that polka dotted the Sawtooth range. The forest service boys called in their locations, updated reports, and requested supplies. Sometimes they called to chat up a feminine voice.

Dick was a frequent caller. He and Kate were soon on a friendly and first name basis although they had never met. Dick began to sign off with a warning. "There's this no good fellow," Dick told Kate, "comin' to town soon. Goes by the name of Richard Spellman." His voice crackled over the wireless. "Now you watch out for him. He's nothing but trouble." For weeks Kate was reminded to watch for trouble.

One Friday, late in the day, a fellow strode into the office. Dusty from the road, he doffed his hat. A grin split his chiseled face. He wiped his hand on his uniform trousers and offered it in introduction."The name's Richard Spellman," he announced. "Watch out for me. I'm trouble."

Kate knew Dick's voice from the radio. They married just months later.

Dick was ever the prankster. He made it his mission to assure the rite of passage of children, family and friends. When he knew he could rely on an almost or full moon, he collected burlap bags and little guys and gals and took them on a snipe hunt. He wet a finger and tested for wind direction to establish placement of the young hunters so the animals would not catch their scents. Snipes are birds, but the children were somehow convinced they were furry, friendly little rodents. At dusk, holding their bags open just so, the boys and girls made clucking sounds with their tongues which, with practice, were certain to lure the snipes into their gunny sacks. Dick drifted away from the kiddie encampment with promises to persuade any snipes he might come across in the direction of the would be hunters. Many's the kid left holding the bag by moonlight.

Had he known, Mae's husband Henry would never have approved the alcohol in her recipe. Whiskey was kept around the house for medicinal purposes only. Snake bite. But Old Stiff Neck sure did love his mincemeat.

Mae's Mincemeat

1 pound	lean beef or venison, cooked and chopped
½ pound	beef suet, chopped
2 pound	apples
2 cups	sugar
1 pound	currants
1 pound	raisins
1	orange, juice and rind
1	lemon, juice and rind
½ teaspoon	salt
¾ teaspoon	nutmeg
½ teaspoon	cinnamon
1 teaspoon	allspice
1 cup	whiskey, brandy, or rum

Put beef, suet, and apples through a grinder. Place in a large pot or Dutch pot and add sugar, currants, raisins, orange and lemon juice and rind, salt, nutmeg, and cinnamon. Heat almost to a boil and simmer 2 hours.

Cool and stir in whiskey, brandy, or rum.

Pack in a crock or in 2 and 3 cup portions and freeze.

Mincemeat Pie with Double Crust

2 ½ cups	flour
1 teaspoon	salt
2/3 cup	lard
6-8 tablespoons	water
3 cups	mincemeat

Mix the flour and salt. Using a pastry blender or two knives, cut in lard until pieces are about the size of peas. Divide the mixture into about 3 parts within the bowl. Sprinkle 2 tablespoons water over about a third of the flour and lard mixture. Toss gently with a fork until moistened. Push to the side of the bowl. Sprinkle and incorporate the third and fourth tablespoons of water over another third of the flour and lard mixture. Repeat with the last third and 2 tablespoon water. You will need six to eight tablespoons of water.

Form into two balls. Flatten the dough on a lightly floured surface. Using a rolling pin, roll from the center to edges making a 10 to 12 inch circle. Fold into quarters and lift into pie pan. Fill with mincemeat.

Cover with crust and pierce.

Bake at 450° 10 minutes. Then lower temperature to 350° and bake another 25 to 30 minutes. Cool before serving.

You may use any pie crust recipe.

Mincemeat Bar Cookies

2/3 cup	sugar
½ cup	butter, at room temperature
1 cup	flour
¾ cup	rolled oats
¼ cup	chopped nuts
¼ teaspoon	baking soda
¼ teaspoon	salt
2 cups	mincemeat

Preheat oven to 400°.

Grease a 13x9" baking pan.

Cream sugar and butter. Stir in flour, rolled oats, chopped nuts, baking soda, and salt. Mixture will be crumbly. Press two cups of this mixture into pan. Spread mincemeat over. Sprinkle remaining flour mixture over mincemeat and pat down gently.

Bake at 400° for about 20 minutes or until golden brown.

Cool and cut into bar cookies. Makes about 20.

This is also good served as a dessert, warm with whipped cream or ice cream.

For Jam Bars, the two cups of mincemeat can be replaced with two cups jam, any kind.

When Mae was lookin' 'round up at the Golden Rule, she spotted a can of salmon for twenty five cents. Do you have any idee how far you can stretch a pound of salmon? Once you got the nasty skin and bones out, it made a tasty little dish.

Mae's Salmon Cakes

1 pound	salmon, canned, picked through for skin and bones, and flaked
2 cups	cold mashed potatoes
½ cup	finely chopped scallions or grated onion
1 teaspoon	salt
½ teaspoon	pepper
1 teaspoon	sage, dried and crumbled
2 tablespoons	butter, melted and cooled
3	eggs
3 tablespoons	butter

Combine salmon, mashed potatoes, grated onion, salt, pepper, sage, melted butter, and eggs.

Form mixture into patties and fry in about 3 tablespoons butter.

Serves 5-6.

Why may I not love Johnny,
And why may not Johnny love me?
And why may I not love Johnny
As well as another body?

Twenty-three

The Inside Girls

'course I had my worries. I tried to put my worries away in little pockets and take a look see at 'em later. But I didn't have enough pockets for Sada. I fretted most about her never finding a man, she so wanted herself a husband and babies.

Sada

As she grew to young womanhood and saw her sisters marry and have children, Sada seldom felt encouraged to meet eligible young men. At twenty-eight years, the light went out of her eyes when her Daddy died. She consoled her mother as best she could and tried to content herself. She sat quietly and crocheted or embroidered or baked or cared for her young nieces and nephew.

Word was there was a new man in town, down from Washington. He worked at the garage and boasted honest grease under his fingernails. No one was quite sure if he was a widower or divorced, but it did not seem to matter. He was older, a bit on the quiet side, a trifle oafish, and available. Kate and Mae invited him to a family picnic, and he found himself seated across the table from Sada, a huge Dutch oven of chicken between them. Breaking the silence, he cleared his throat and remarked on the weather. Sada, wearing a brave little ribbon in her hair, nodded her head and stared at her plate. Not easily discouraged, he asked a question about her sister, Mae. Sada answered her plate. Finally, he asked her to please pass the butter for his bread and he managed to catch her eyes. She smiled as prettily as she knew how, and she was astonished to find she could actually look at him. She found that instead of becoming flustered and red faced and forgetting her words, she could actually talk to this man. She all but ignored the nieces who clamored for her attention, and she chatted with Ollie Bell until her jaws hurt. Her mother and sisters were agog. *Glory be!* The girl could talk.

The light came back in her eyes. Ollie was captivated and his intentions were honorable. Much to the delight of her sisters, Sada and Ollie were married just after her thirty-eighth birthday. They stayed on at the ranch so Mary Ann never really lost her embroidering partner. Some years later, Ollie moved Sada into a tiny house in town. There was a barn on the little city lot, so Sada had her cats. She kept chickens in the yard, baked to her heart's content, and she *paid no never mind* to the dust kittens lurking beneath her furniture.

Sada had all but given up hope of ever having a husband and home. Immersed in happiness, she began to have new dreams. She so wanted to give Ollie a child. Truth be told, over the years Sada had so many miscarriages, her mother and sisters wondered if she reckoned each monthly stain as yet another lost babe. The family finally lost count. Sada never did.

Edna

One year, Edna accompanied Mary Ann on her winter trip to Los Angeles. Not one to sit about when there was work to be done, Edna applied for a waitressing job at the lunch counter of a local drug store. Her mornings were free, so she stayed around the house, helped Elmo, and looked after her little niece and nephew.

The breadman dressed in his snappy blue and yellow uniform zigged and zagged his little yellow and blue van through the morning neighborhoods of Los Angeles. Little Rae and Denny raced out the front door at the sound of his sharp whistle, Edna right behind them. She looked over the fresh loaves of bread and coffee cakes and doughnuts and took her own sweet time to make a decision. While she and the breadman played googly eyes, he kept the children in jelly doughnuts. The little ones wondered if she got up early to visit with the nice milk man, and they wished she would strike up a friendship with the afternoon ice cream man as well.

Edna went home to Idaho and lived awhile with her sister Katie. She took a job as a waitress in a restaurant in Salmon where she met a nice guitar *pickin'* Idaho man, born and bred. Apparently Edna liked a man in uniform. She served up a blue plate special to Bill LaMunyan who sported postal blues. All in good time they married and gave Mary Ann two dear little grandsons, Larry and Steve. After all those silly girls, grandboys were such fun.

Sada's Sausage and Sweet Spud Hash

4	large sweet potatoes, peeled and chunked
1 pound	pork sausage
2	onions, chopped
1 teaspoon	cinnamon
1 tablespoon	dried sage
	salt and pepper

Set a pot of water to boiling. Cook the sweet potatoes in boiling, salted water about 15 to 20 minutes or until tender. Drain.

Cook the sausage in a skillet just until it starts to brown. Add the onions and continue cooking until the sausage is crumbly and browned and the onions are translucent. Add the sweet potatoes and cinnamon. Cook about 10 more minutes. Rub the sage between your palms over the meat and vegetables. Salt and pepper to taste.

Serves 8.

Edna's Cherry Nut Cupcakes

½ cup	butter
1 ¼ cups	sugar
2	eggs, beaten
1 cup	sour cream
2 ½ cups	flour
1 teaspoon	baking soda
1 teaspoon	nutmeg
1 cup	pie cherries, pitted and drained
1 cup	walnuts, broken

Preheat oven to 325°. Prepare muffin tins with grease and flour or 2 dozen cupcake liners.

Cream butter and sugar. Stir in eggs and sour cream. Combine flour, baking soda, and nutmeg and add to creamed mixture. Fold in cherries and walnuts.

Drop by large spoonsful into muffin tins.

Bake at 325° 25 to 30 minutes.

Makes about two dozen.

There was an old woman
Lived under the hill,
And if she's not gone
She lives there still.

Twenty-four

Home Sweet Homes

Mary Ann awoke to a peaches and cream day. Shades of palest orange and pink painted the eastern sky and reflected off a bank of whipped cream clouds.

I grabbed my hat and my hoe and headed for my garden. I spotted a rabbit gnawing on my plant babies. I ran to shoo him and I twisted my ankle and took a terrible spill. Busted my knee up somethin' awful, bled right through my skirt. I picked myself up and limped back up to the house. Bleedin' and breathless, I knew I'd be needin' iodine and a clean rag for my sorry leg.

I was a bundle of black and blue, but lookin' back it probably wasn't so bad. I could have broke my wrists. My knee took its own sweet time to heal and was ever after a bit gimpy. That tumble was what I needed to decide me it was time to let the ranch go. My outside girls had done a grand job of keeping it a goin'. Katie held her own with the haying crews and Mae came up and pitched in when she could. Without someone to oversee, it was just too much for me. I was just gettin' too old. I had my chats with the girls. Even though Sada and Ollie was livin' with me, they didn't want to take over the spread. It was time to sell. The girlies promised me beds at their places. I had homes to go to and God blessed me with grandchildren to visit, four boys and three girls. My girlies helped me divide and store the trinkets I wasn't ready to part with and we parked my pride and joy piano at Mae's. So I began my comin's and goin's.

Mary Ann learned to travel light with only two ancient leather valises. The first few years, she had Kate and Edna in tow. One year, during the war, Mary Ann stayed with Irma and Frank while their daughters went to Salt Lake City with Kate and Edna. The youngest, Jeannie, went to beauty school while Mary and her aunts found jobs. The foursome had an apartment with one double bed, a hot plate, and a shared bathroom down the hall. They slept crosswise on the bed, and when one turned over they all had to shift. They were sardines layered in a can.

As Thanksgiving approached, the girls realized they could not go home to Hailey as they all had to be at work or school the next day. They set about making the best Thanksgiving they knew how in their one room apartment with the hotplate, a fry pan, and a kettle. The shopping and jobs were spoken for. Jeannie was to buy a can of olives. Now, olives were a considered a rare treat. Mary Ann served olives for Easter, Thanksgiving, Christmas, and the occasional picnic. As the girls sat about their tiny table, enjoying the fruits of their labor, Katie spit an olive seed across the table at Mary. Soon the pits were flying. Mae's husband, Henry, whom they lovingly called Old Stiff Neck, disliked the family tradition of shooting olive seeds. He even made a fuss about *such goin's on* when they were on picnics. The girls got to laughing about Henry and family times and gatherings. They laughed until they cried, then they bawled. They discovered olive pits around the tiny apartment for days.

At Irma and Frank's ranch, Mary Ann helped with garden, the kitchen, and the laundry. Sada and Ollie always welcomed her as did Mae and Henry. She could always find something to do. She baked her feathery biscuits and tasty pies. At the very least, she folded laundry and went after a weed or two. She spent a few weeks here, a month there, and did her helpful best to keep out of the way. When husbands came home, she scampered off to her room and read a chapter or two of one of her western romances. She knew how to make herself scarce, and she felt it was important to give a family private time to catch up on the day.

Winters were difficult for Mary Ann in Idaho. She never wanted to miss the festivities of Thanksgiving and Christmas, but when the bitter cold of January set in, she was ready to go south to Elmo and Emil's in Los Angeles. She thrived in the sunshine, weathered the few rainy days, and enjoyed her walks. Elmo was pleased to spoil the mother who had worked hard, made do, and gone without the frills in life. They lunched out, made junkets to the beach, visited rose gardens and museums, and shopped. When Mary Ann stayed at Elmo's, Little Denny was booted from the bedroom and Little Rae became Mary Ann's overwinter roommate. Early on, Mary Ann discovered some similarities between her daughter Katie and her granddaughter, Naughty Rae. The little whippersnapper had an especially quick and wicked tongue, so Mary Ann took to carrying a touch of black spice in her apron pocket for just the right occasion. All in good time another tiny tongue was tamed with good intentions and a sprinkle of pepper.

Mary Ann and her little granddaughter pestered each other over this and squabbled over that. Except for the difference in years, they might have been sisters. Mary Ann took over two drawers when she visited, and one year Little Rae went snooping. Hidden under her grandmother's pale peach panties she spied a box of chocolate covered orange sticks. Naughty Little Rae took to pilfering a few here and there. She thought her grandmother would never notice. Not a word was said. When Mary Ann departed for Idaho, she usually left silver dollars in the two drawers, one for each of the children. That year, Denny got his silver dollar.

Whenever I went for my visit, I'd pitch in where I could. Except for my biscuits and pies, Elmo's husband didn't take much to my brand of cookin'. "Too much gravy," he said. So mostly I ended up doin' dishes. They'd all be sittin' 'round the table talkin' and I was hankerin' to get them dishes done so's I could watch their teleevision. Sometimes I'd grab a dish off the table before they was done. I'd wash and Little Rae would dry. My stars! That little girly took such pleasure in findin' I'd missed a spot on a dish, and she'd give it a toss back in my dishwater.

When Katie and Dick married and moved to Salmon, Mary Ann had a brand new house and territory to explore. Her great grandson Gene got his driver's license some years later. Ever on the lookout for a ride here or there, Mary Ann hit Gene up for a lift to Salmon so Katie could do her hair. Gene tried to explain he had plans for a hunting trip, but Mary Ann would hear none of it. Gene finally surrendered to her coaxing and off they went. They left at six in the morning and expected to pull up to the Spellman house about lunch time. Slamming around a corner on the highway, they came within inches of hitting a black bear as he sunned himself on the pavement. Mary Ann commented on what good time they were making. They arrived about ten thirty. Katie and her mother calculated the miles and time and were aghast. Gene had made the six hour trip in four and a half hours. Mary Ann kept her eyes on the speedometer the entire trip home.

Edna and Bill's home provided yet another happy place to be. Their boys, Larry and Steve, kept Mary Ann on her toes. She babysat them, helped around the house, and enjoyed time and memories with her Edna as they crocheted and embroidered together. Mary Ann always kept her hands busy. *Idle hands are the devil's hands.* When her eyes started to go, she learned to knit afghans on huge needles.

Leftover Pies for Supper

Set oven at 350°.

Using the recipe for Mary Ann's Lard Pie Crust or Butter Pie Crust, divide and roll out dough circles and fill with sweets or savories to make turnover style pies. Fill, fold in half, crimp edges, and bake.

Sweets may include chopped fruit, cream cheese, jam, nuts, sweetened with a little honey or brown sugar and cinnamon. Dust crust with sugar.

Savories may include chopped cooked meats or sausage, cheese, tomatoes, scrambled eggs, beans or corn with a little salt and pepper and sage. Dust crust with salt.

Bake at 350° for 20-25 minutes or until golden.

Katie's Sourdough Waffles

1 cup	sourdough starter
2 cups	warm water
3 cups	flour
1 teaspoon	dry yeast

The night before you are planning to bake, put your starter, the warm water, the flour, and yeast in a mixing bowl. Mix and put one cup of the starter back in the crock. Leave the crock and the covered bowl at room temperature over night.

1	egg
1 t.	salt
2 t.	baking powder
3 T.	sugar
¼ c.	oil

To the sourdough mixture in the bowl, add eggs, salt, baking powder, sugar, and oil. If mixture seems too runny, add a little more flour. Stir only enough to combine and try not to destroy sourdough bubbles.

Ladle and bake on a hot waffle iron.

Makes 10 or so, depending on size of the waffle iron.

Mister East gave a feast.
Mister North laid the cloth.
Mister West did his best.
Mister South burnt his mouth
Eating cold potato.

Twenty-five

Picnic Sundays

If I had a nickel for every picnic memory, I could pad my pocketbook. Sundays we'd be gathering with my sister Maudie, Ray and their folks. As our family grew all comers were on the invite. Ever'one brought a Dutch oven chicken, a casserole, a salad, and a dessert. We all had our favorites to bring and our favorites to eat. If Maudie forgot her spud salad she'd hear about it all the day. We'd nestle bottles of sodee pop in the creek. Gracious how a sodee could mend a parched throat. Most times, as long as the ice was lasting, someone brought along the ice cream. The little ones would take turns at the crank until it became too hard. Then they'd give it over to a growed up for the final work of it. There was nothing like the taste of homemade ice cream to top off a piece of pie or cake or a picnic.

The gatherings began in Carey, moved to Mackay, and finally up East Fork of the Little Wood River. As the family had more access to cars and roads improved, the get togethers moved up to Sunbeam where the hot springs mixed with the cool waters of the Salmon River. They found favorite spots up Trail Creek, over Galena, up to Stanley, and Red Fish Lake. A Sunday in summer was the only excuse needed to gather the Ivie clan for a picnic.

Some of the menfolk would scurry up a game of horseshoes although most were content to sit around swapping lies. A few of the fellows would take themselves off some paces to share a beer or a tipple of bourbon and an off color joke. Alcohol was not tolerated at the picnic proper. The gals covered the tables with a collection of cloths and displayed their contributions. Casseroles and salads marched down the center of the tables where the folks would sit to eat while the desserts typically tempted from their very own table. The womenfolk arranged and chatted and reviewed the gossip of pregnancies, gall bladders, wayward children, and who had been seen with whom. Youngsters chased and yelled, played hide and seek, waded and caught minnows, fetched firewood, pitched pup tents for the naps that rarely happened, and dreamed of water fights later in the day. Scoldings were few and far between. Kids were bound to get wet and dirty, and mothers came prepared with changes of clothing.

Everyone settled in come time to eat. Chicken was the mainstay, but the other choices, *my stars!* You could piece here, eat there, and never sample the same dish twice. Salads were a favorite. In winter, folks just didn't buy such as lettuce and tomatoes, even if they were available. They were far too dear in price. The closest anyone came to salad in wintry weather was a withered hunk of cabbage tossed up as slaw. So when the pretty fresh salads made their summer appearances at picnics, they vanished with all manner of dressings before the blink of an eye.

After dinner clean up found Mary Ann caught in the act of collecting the used plastic picnic ware. She was astounded at the waste of tossing *perfectly good* plastic spoons and forks and cups at end of day. She would bag them along with gently used plates, take them home, wash them, and fetch them to the next reunion. *Waste not, want not.*

The fun and frolic began with the spitting of olive seeds at table. Although some of the adults did not approve, they usually turned a blind eye at a picnic. Mirth and mayhem escalated when, after dinner, huge wedges of watermelon were passed around. Every kid was eager to spit a few seeds to see how far they might go and where they might land.

The climax of an Ivie picnic was the water fight. There were three levels of participation. The instigators took front and center. Katie and Mary, eldest daughter of Irma and Frank, were the captains with Rod, son of Mae and Henry, as their first lieutenant. Followers included all the kids. The innocent bystanders had more than an inkling of the sport to come.

There were three rules. Get everyone wet as possible. Steer clear of the dessert table. Avoid getting the oldsters. The first and second rules were the only ones heeded. No one liked a soggy brownie.

Everyone knew to keep Mary Ann dry. That lasted for a pair of seconds. After her first dousing, she would sputter and steam. She sat almost regally on her campstool, all a drip. Soon chortling, she commissioned any child willing to do her bidding to bring her a cup of water so she was prepared for the next assault. One year she surprised her attacker when she drew a water pistol from her pocket and fired. Water guns had been outlawed, but after Mary Ann's unexpected foray, the rules changed forever.

Bone weary, soaked, happy at end of day, the families departed for home. Children sported a few cuts and bruises, trophies of the time. They were ready for baths and beds. Henry came home from a Sunday picnic and declared himself saddle sore from riding with his brother in law, Frank, all day. Frank's stories of cowboying on the range plum tuckered everyone out.

Before day's end, the next picnic destination was determined. The Ivie and Knight and Brasse and Bell and Erlandson and Spellman and LaMunyan picnics held special moments and memories. Moments did not last, but the memories did. In the midst of an Idaho summer's beauty and bounty, it was difficult to remember that fall was just around the corner with winter nipping at its heels.

Mary Ann's Ideeho Fried Dutch Oven Chicken

2 cups	fat for frying
1	chicken, cut up
1 cup	buttermilk
¾ cup	flour
1 tablespoon	salt
1 tablespoon	sage
1 tablespoon	pepper

Soak chicken pieces in buttermilk for about 30 minutes.

In a Dutch oven or cast iron fry pan, heat the oil until it sizzles a drop of water.

In a paper bag, combine flour, salt, sage, and pepper. Drop two or three pieces of chicken into the bag and shake to coat. Place pieces on a plate for a minute or two to allow them to dry. Fry meatier pieces first, and do not crowd them. Add smaller pieces and brown for about 15 minutes. Reduce heat, cover and cook 30 to 35 minutes. Uncover and cook about 10 more minutes to crisp.

When taken to a picnic in a Dutch oven, the chicken was fully cooked (the original 30 to 35 minutes.) The oven was set by the fire to heat through, turned, then uncovered for the last 10 minutes to crisp.

Katie's Sausage, Cabbage, and Noodles

½ pound	sausage
½ cup	butter
1	head of cabbage, thinly sliced
	noodles
1 tablespoon	salt
1 teaspoon	pepper

Brown sausage in a Dutch oven or large pot. Remove sausage and set aside. Add enough butter to the oil to make about ½ cup. Drop cabbage into the heated oil and butter and cook slowly, 30 to 40 minutes. Cook noodles in another pot and drain. Combine cabbage, noodles, and sausage and season with salt and pepper.

Serves 6 to 8.

Noodles

2 cups	flour
3	eggs
2 tablespoons	water
1 teaspoon	salt

Combine flour, eggs, water, and salt. Dough will be stiff. Turn out on a floured board and knead. Roll out into a large, thin sheet. Generously sprinkle with flour and roll up as if making a jelly roll. Slice across the roll to make noodles.

Shake out, shake off excess flour, and lay out to dry, at least an hour. Noodles may be dropped into simmering water or broth a few at time and cooked 15 to 20 minutes.

Maudie's Spud Salad

6	slices bacon
1/3 cup	vinegar
2 tablespoons	water
1	egg, beaten
1 teaspoon	sugar
1 teaspoon	salt
½ teaspoon	pepper
6 cups	potatoes, peeled, cooked, and diced
½ cup	scallions, chopped

Fry bacon, cool, crumble. Set aside. To warm bacon drippings, add vinegar, water, egg, sugar, salt, and pepper. Heat and stir until thick. Toss potatoes with the warm dressing, crumbled bacon, and scallions.

Serve warm or cold.

Serves 8-10.

See a pin and pick it up,
All the day you'll have good luck.
See a pin and let it lay,
You will have bad luck all day.

Twenty-six

Thunder Mug

When I was thinking on my own home and playin' house with my Dear Alden, my sweet Mama 'most ruined the whole daydream. She ordered me up a chamber pot from the catalogue. That brought a girl to her senses quick, let me tell you. I recollect emptyin' and cleanin' that pot was the very worst memory of my home keeping.

Mary Ann was strict with her family as to why and when they might use the inside facilities instead of making the necessary march to the privy. She had visited her father in California and enjoyed the comforts of an inside toilet. She had luxuriated in a bath where she could submerge her entire body. She ever after *honeyed* her husband to provide such luxuries, but the closest she ever got to genteel in her own home was an inside pump for water. It was a true back and time saver, but she had to wait until her girls were married and on their own to enjoy a real bathroom.

Shared though it was, her first true bathroom was at Mae and Henry's, up East Fork. Her favorite, though, was at Elmo's in Los Angeles. Peach tile, a huge tub, a large mirror, and a separate shower stall made her feel almost the queen, even if she had to share with four other bodies.

In her later years, Mary Ann had occasion to participate in a community potluck supper to which she brought one of her famous cakes. A young matron thought she had quite the find of the century. It was, she claimed, an antique serving vessel.

189

Enormous, it was just the right size to present her lovely chicken and noodles. The oldsters chuckled and clicked their tongues and steered clear of the young woman's contribution. *For certain sure*, they would not eat anything from someone's old piddle pot.

Chicken and noodles was always welcomed at a potluck, 'course in a proper pot.

Irma's Chicken and Noodles

1	chicken, cut up
4 quarts	water
2	onions, diced
2 cups	celery, diced
2 cups	carrots, diced
2 cups	corn
2-3 cups	potatoes, diced
1 tablespoon	salt
½ teaspoon	pepper
1 teaspoon	sage, rubbed between palms over soup

Place chicken in a large Dutch oven or soup pot and cover with water. Bring to boil and simmer until tender, about one hour.

Remove chicken from heat and allow to cool. Take meat from the bones and cut into bite sized pieces. Discard skin and bones. Skim the fat as the broth cools and discard. Return broth to a simmer and add vegetables and chicken pieces, salt, pepper, and sage. Simmer about 15 minutes.

Add noodles and simmer about 15 minutes more.

Noodles

2 cups	flour
3	eggs
2 tablespoons	water
1 teaspoons	salt

Combine flour, eggs, water, and salt. Dough will be stiff. Turn out on a floured board and knead. Roll out into a large, thin sheet. Generously sprinkle with flour and roll up as if making a jelly roll. Slice across the roll to make noodles. Shake out, shake off excess flour, and lay out to dry, at least an hour.

Noodles may be dropped into the simmering broth a few at time and cook 15 to 20 minutes.

I like my noodles thick and wide. They shouldn't look store bought.

Mary Ann's Lazy Cake

1	egg
½ cup	sugar
1 cup	flour
1 teaspoon	baking powder
pinch	salt
¼ cup	milk or top milk
3 tablespoons	butter, melted and cooled
1 teaspoon	vanilla

Preheat oven to 350°. Grease and flour an 8" or 9" round pan.

Beat egg until fluffy. Add sugar while beating. Add remaining ingredients while continuing to beat. Pour into pan. Drop pan about three inches onto counter to bring air bubbles to the top.

Bake at 350° 25 minutes. Cool and turn out on plate.

Frost with whipped cream and top with fruit.

Curly locks, curly locks
Will you be mine?
You shall not wash clothes
Nor yet feed the swine.
But sit on a cushion
And sew a fine seam
And feed upon strawberries
Sugar and cream.

Twenty-seven

Strawberries

I was seventy and something when I woke up to all over hives. They was in my ears, on my eyelids, and under my finger nails. I thought to die of the itchin' and my only relief was a bath of baking soda and cool water in Elmo's big tub. The doctor said it was most likely something I ate and the red welts would disappear all in good time. I was purely miserable.

When Mary Ann and Alden moved to their own little spot in Carey, her mother gifted them with strawberry starts for their garden. Mary Ann tended and weeded and watered those tender shoots during the first growing season, and the next year she had berries a plenty to eat fresh, to cook, and to jam. When Mary Ann moved to Mackay and then on to Hailey, she took her strawberry starts along. She so loved their fragrance, color, sweetness and the memories they brought of her Sweet Mama, Maria.

The spring she awoke with hives, she was with her daughter in Los Angeles. Elmo's doctor suggested oatmeal baths. They helped some, but to be certain of sleep, Mary Ann's son-in-law poured her two fingers of bourbon before she went to bed each night. She became so dependent upon her *sleepy medicine*, she decided to stay with Kate and Dick when she returned to Idaho later in the spring. She knew Dick would pour her *medicine*. Mae's husband, Henry, would not tolerate the evil stuff in his house, except perhaps to cure snakebite.

The hives abated as summer ended, and she almost forgot her miseries. Then she was off to Los Angeles for another winter. About the first of March, she was horrified to find the itchy blotches again covered her body like so much red chenille. Perhaps she was allergic to California or to her roommate, Little Rae.

Elmo took her mother to a specialist who concluded it was a food allergy. He put her on an elimination diet. For six weeks, Mary Ann could have nothing but lamb chops, steamed white rice, and tea. Thereafter she was to slowly add back other foods until the culprit was discovered.

May was a busy month with Elmo's birthday, Denny's birthday, and Mother's Day. Mary Ann adored being fussed over. Elmo spoiled her with lunches out, shopping for a new spring frock, and a big dinner on Sunday.

At the end of the meal, Little Rae marched in with a lovely strawberry rhubarb cake. Mary Ann happily tucked away two helpings.

Next morning she awoke as crimson as the strawberries she had consumed the evening before. She shook her head in disgust. She decided to be happy she had been able to enjoy those juicy red tidbits for a good seventy years. Knowing how she relished them, her daughters took care not to serve the tempting fruit when she was about. She never ate another strawberry.

Mary Ann's Baked Strawberry Custard

2 teaspoons	butter
2 cups	strawberries, cleaned and sliced in half
1 tablespoon	cornstarch
3	eggs
1 cup	milk or ½ cup milk and ½ cup cream
2/3 cup	flour
1/3 to ½ cup	sugar, depending on the sweetness of the berries
2 teaspoons	vanilla
pinch	salt

Preheat oven to 350°.

Grease a 2 quart baking dish with butter.

Toss strawberries with cornstarch and place cut side down in dish.

Beat together eggs, milk, flour, sugar, vanilla, and salt. Pour over strawberries.

Bake at 350° for 45-50 minutes or until golden brown and puffy. Serve warm.

Serves 6-8

Elmo's Strawberry Rhubarb Cake

2 cups	flour
2 teaspoons	soda
½ teaspoon	salt
1 teaspoon	nutmeg
1 cup	strawberries, crushed
½ cup	buttermilk
3	eggs
1¾ cups	sugar
2 tablespoons	butter, melted and cooled
3½ cups	rhubarb, finely chopped

Preheat oven to 375°.

Grease and flour a 9x13 inch pan or two 8 inch round pans.

Combine flour, soda, salt, and nutmeg in a small bowl. In a larger bowl, combine strawberries, buttermilk, eggs, sugar, and butter. Fold in dry ingredients, then fold in rhubarb. Pour into greased and floured pan or pans. Drop pan about three inches on to counter to bring air bubbles to the top.

Bake at 375° 30 to 35 minutes or until done in center for 13x9 inch pan or 25 to 30 minutes for 8 inch pans.

Cool completely before topping.

Serves 12 – 16.

Cake Topping

1 cup	whipping cream
1 tablespoon	sugar
1 teaspoon	vanilla

Whip cream with sugar and add vanilla. Spread over cooled cake.
Serves 12-16.

Twenty-eight

Empty Apron Pockets

There is a sweet little spot on the Salmon River at Sunbeam Hot Springs. Many years ago, folks fashioned little tubs of rocks to temporarily hold the waters. Mary Ann doffed her clothes right down to her bathing costume and picked her way over the rocks to find her very own stone ringed pool. She nestled in as the waters blended and the temperature felt just right. She reclined, closed her eyes, and reflected on the mix of her life. The happy times and sad times balanced much as the waters mingled. She had to feel the cold in order to enjoy the warmth just as she had to bear sadness so that she would rejoice in happiness. Her reveries were interrupted by the splash and dash of a fellow bather. It was time to go and get on with the day.

One day my girlies, Kate and Mae and Sada, sat me down, poured me a cup of tea, sweetened the deal with an applesass cookie or two, and asked me the big question. They wanted to know if I had a plan or wishes for my funeral when it was my time to pass. At first I was a little upsetted, but their question tickled my funny bone. I sipped my tea, munched my cookie, and said, "Why don't you just surprise me?"

At day's end, Mary Ann emptied her apron pockets and looked through the collection of odds and ends and treasures she found there. Buttons to the button box, bits of string to the twine ball that grew in the kitchen, safety and straight pins to the pin cushion, hair pins to the old chipped saucer she kept on her dresser, a nickel to her penny jar. She sorted her day and threw her apron on the wash pile. She would wear a fresh apron tomorrow.

We had us some good times and we had us some bad times.
I learned early on to remember the good and forget the bad.
I did the best I knowed.
Mary Ann Ivie
1878-1972

Epilogue

Little Grandma

My sixteenth summer, I was elected to take Grandma from Los Angeles back to Idaho. Almost eighty one, the family considered her far too frail to be traveling alone. I approached the junket with mixed feelings. A few days in Idaho with my aunts and uncles and cousins would be fun, but a trip by bus with Grandma was bound to be taxing. That little old gal turned out to be nothing but fun once we waved goodbye to her daughter, my mother. We had ourselves a grand time as we swapped stories. It was one big slumber party, and we talked all night. She told me things she swore she had never shared with anyone but God and her sister, Maudie.

We reached Reno about eight the next morning. As we freshened up in the bus stop restroom, Grandma asked what I was going to order for breakfast. Never much of a breakfast eater, I answered "A cheeseburger and french fries."

My grandmother was aghast. "Well, I never! That's not a proper breakfast!"

When we left the restroom headed for the lunch counter, we had to run the gauntlet between rows of one armed bandits. As we neared the last machine Grandma paused and produced four nickels from her pocketbook. She slid the first nickel into the slot, closed her eyes, and pulled. She dreamed of jackpot but would have been tickled with a show of cherries. Four coins, four pulls, no wins. She shrugged her shoulders, gave her little pocketbook a pat, and moved on to breakfast.

We were seated. I gave the menu a quick glance although I'd set my mind on a burger. Grandma reminded me to remove my elbows from the table.

When the waitress came to take our order, Grandma couldn't hide her grin. "I'll have a cheeseburger and fried spuds."

The Author

RaeAnn Proost lives in Redmond, Oregon with her husband, Gary. She resides not too far from her daughters and their families in Portland. A retired schoolteacher, RaeAnn served as a writing coach to her students and peers for twenty-six years.

Memories and extensive research led to the writing of PEPPER IN HER POCKET.

A note from the author

At a book signing, a woman asked how I came to write my first book, SORRY LITTLE SUPPER. In an effort to keep it brief, I told her I felt compelled to write the first story because of a series of events that lead to the recycling of a tablecloth my Swedish grandmother had made. The entire book began with one incident and that story became the prologue and epilogue for the finished piece.

Now, the woman had wanted to write family stories, but she didn't know how to begin. I suggested she think of a story that quite possibly no one else in her family knew. Then I said, "If you don't write the story, who will?"

Tears welled in her eyes. Her voice caught in her throat as she said, "No one." She went on to say that no one would ever know about her grandmother who had crossed the plains to Oregon. No one would know about the abandoned house the parents discovered and settled into. No one would know that when she, a small girl, brought in an armful of kindling to start the fire, a rattlesnake slithered out of the fireplace and into the room. No one would know how she shooed it out the door and laid the fire for the family's first dinner in their little adopted house. No one.

I hope she went home and put that story to paper for her children and grandchildren. If she doesn't, who will?

If the telling of your family stories is up to you, you might begin with an old photograph or recipe. Write the first draft with your heart, then edit with your head.

I propose to compile a collection of stories for a third book, MORE SORRY LITTLE SUPPERS, THE STOVES AND STORIES OF OUR FAMILIES. If you have a story intertwined with a recipe you would like to share for possible publication in this forthcoming collection, please copy the story (500 to 1500 words) and the recipe to an email (no attachments, please.) Please send it to me before December 31, 2008 at sorrylittlesupper@bendbroadband.com. In the event your story and recipe become part of the final publication, you will receive an honorarium.

If you don't, who will?

RaeAnn Proost
2007

Photographs from the Ivie Family Archives

Printed in the United States
98301LV00003B/316-366/A

9 781601 453167